Challenging Voices

*Writings by, for, and About
Individuals with
Learning Disabilities*

Cheryl Gerson Tuttle, M.Ed.
and
Gerald A. Tuttle, Ph.D.

With a Foreword by William Ellis

Library of Congress Cataloging-in-Publication Data

Tuttle, Cheryl Gerson.
    Challenging voices : writings by, for, and about individuals
with learning disabilities / Cheryl Gerson Tuttle and Gerald A.
Tuttle.
      p. cm.
    ISBN 1-56565-211-8
    1. Learning disabled, Writings of the, American. 2. Learning
disabilities—United States—Literary collections. 3. Learning
disabled—United States—Literary collections. 4. American
literature—20th century. I. Tuttle, Gerald A. II. Title.
PS508.L43T87 1995
 810.8'092826—dc20   94-25173
                                       CIP

Requests for such permissions should be addressed to:
Lowell House
2029 Century Park East, Suite 3290
Los Angeles, CA 90067

Lowell House books can be purchased at special discounts when ordered in
bulk for premiums and special sales. Contact Department VH at the address
above.

Publisher: Jack Artenstein
General Manager, Lowell House Adult: Bud Sperry
Text Design: Susan H. Hartman

Manufactured in the United States of America
10 9 8 7 6 5 4 3 2 1

For Matthew and Ross

Contents

Foreword

William Ellis
Executive Editor, Their World,
A Publication of the National
Center for Learning Disabilities

Learning disabilities have human faces. They come in many shapes and sizes. Their reality shows itself in the actual lives and experiences of individuals with learning disabilities. It seems obvious, but in spite of everything that we now know, and it is plenty, there is still hostility toward the idea that these disabilities are easily corrected if the individual would only apply him or herself. Hidden handicaps are not easily revealed to the non-discerning, the skeptical, or the blatant nonbeliever. There is every reason to applaud Cheryl and Gerald Tuttle for putting together this collection of writings and every reason to congratulate the writers, all of whom have given a compelling picture of the reality of learning disabilities.

And the picture hangs proudly with its subtle shades and textures, not always visible until you get near the canvas and look closely. When we allow ourselves to see, we find that parts of this remarkable design are fraught with potential problems and dilemmas which, when not properly attended to, create a less-inspiring whole and do not do justice to each of the elements which create the final effect of the picture. Learning disabilities are like that. They create the possibility of diminishing all of us. They mask the potency of each individual's contribution and the majesty of the community to which we all belong.

That's why this book is so important. It's hard to walk in someone else's shoes. We often don't know even where to find them. Our interest in the topic of learning disabilities is sometimes lopsided or even abstract. This book connects us to the reality, and it is done with the grace, humor, feeling, power, and genuineness which only those who live it can truly express. We now know so much more than we did, even when many of these writers began their journey into this fascinating world. Too often we are far behind acting on what we actually know. It is much easier to live with the status quo than to renew our energies with the latest knowledge. Anyone reading this book will find their spirits and consequently their energies renewed.

Acknowledgments

We would like to thank the many children, young adults, adults, parents, grandparents, sisters, and brothers who agreed to contribute to this work. Without their cooperation and participation, there would be no book. These individuals are listed in appendix A.

We especially thank the many national and local organizations, schools, and publications that recognized our vision for this book. They generously passed on our requests and encouraged their friends and students to share their writings. These organizations and schools are listed in appendix B.

Most of all, we thank our family and friends for their support and encouragement, especially Arlene B. Hirschfelder, Lynne Pollack, Esther Levine, and Penny Paquette.

Introduction

Children with learning disabilities have the potential to become successful adults, or so they are told. Famous figures who have overcome their disabilities to become great contributors to society—Albert Einstein, George Patton, and Thomas Edison, to name a few—are often, perhaps too often, cited as examples. History, however, is of little comfort to the child or parent who endures the frustration, pain, and loneliness associated with a learning disability. The successes of Einstein, Patton, and Edison are too remote from the situations children with learning disabilities face every day.

Children with learning disabilities know how they feel today, are concerned about what is happening *now*, and have no idea what the future will bring. Their concerns are real and need to be acknowledged in order for these individuals to grow into healthy adults.

Many children with learning disabilities can express their feelings in writing; indeed, many are gifted writers. They give voice to the millions who cannot or do not write. They help the reader understand what it feels like to be inside their heads, to see the world through their eyes, and to experience their pain and joy.

Challenging Voices is a compilation of essays and poems from across the United States, written by children with learning disabilities as well as by members of their families. Each work reveals a part of their world. Many of these writings specifically address what it is like to grow up with a learning disability, whereas others are observations and impressions that may bear no relation to learning disabilities. In the former group of writings, readers may note a degree of redundancy. The message is often the same, whether written by contributors from California, Oklahoma, Indiana, or Massachusetts. The repetition of ideas and emotions only emphasizes the scope of the problem and the reality of the pain and frustration.

Unfortunately, there are still many who do not believe that learning disabilities and attention deficits exist. Because these handicaps are less visible than physical handicaps, they are more difficult for others to perceive and understand. A person who gets to school in a wheelchair is applauded, whereas a person who has difficulty getting organized receives no such recognition for simply getting to school.

The writings in this book bear testament to the fact that a learning disability is not just an excuse for not trying. These individuals have to try harder than others to achieve the same goals, although this may not be obvious to the casual observer. Robert Lane, a creative writing teacher at the Kildonan School in Amenia, New York, expresses this message beautifully in his poem, "An Abstract Apology":

> Reading this will be hard for you
> not because of what it says, but
> because of what it is;
> letters,
> sounds,
> words,
>
> Words you cannot read as well as I.
>
> Words harsher than
> stupid
> or lazy and dumb.
>
> Not words like god and dog
> or deny.

Words which are   all
                over
                                     the
page
like lost sheep
bleating to deaf ears.

These words cannot
be divided
into syllables,
or ruled
by concepts and
someday conquered.

For these words are
dyslexic words
like help
like hope
like try
it
again.

The children and adults whose writings are included in this book are the brave ones. It takes courage to bare your soul and share your innermost thoughts. Their words are eye-opening and heartwarming. The poems and essays are presented here as written; spelling has been corrected only if the correction does not alter the message. Names mentioned in the writings have been changed or abbreviated, but most authors' names are displayed boldly and proudly. Brief biographical statements about the authors follow some of the writings. These establish that the capabilities and accomplishments of these individuals are indeed significant and are often as "telling" as their compositions.

In addition to the obvious frustration and despair, the writings display humor, hope, imagination, creativity, and intelligence. Each writer is unique and opens himself or herself in the hope of providing encouragement to those who are experiencing similar difficulties and offering understanding to those who question. As one contributor, Margaret Birch, states, "I just want to say to anyone with a learning disability . . . to believe in yourself and to draw from your strengths. If you do this, you can stand on your own two feet. You can overcome any obstacles that may come your way. I want everyone to know I'm proud of my accomplishments and am very happy with my life."

The chapters that follow begin with the writings of young children, then progress through adolescence to adulthood, demonstrating an increasing level of sophistication and perception. The next to the last chapter consists of writings of family members and shows the impact a child with a disability has on every member of the family. It is not necessary to read the book from cover to cover or in any particular order. Pick it up when you need encouragement and support and read those sections that speak to your need. Read it to and with your child. Use it as a catalyst for discussion. Give a copy to your child's teacher, friends, and grandparents—anyone who might be judgmental. They aren't likely to get the book for themselves because they won't know they need to read it!

If you are moved by the writings in this book, the writers have succeeded. If you feel you are not alone, the writers have succeeded. Please listen to their voices—voices that challenge the world to accept them as they are and help them grow and accept themselves.

Chapter 1

Children's Voices

P arents often are concerned about how their child will feel if the child is told he or she has a learning disability. As you can see from these poems and essays, these children don't have to be told. They already know. They look around, as all children do, and compare themselves with others. These comparisons begin early. Giving these youngsters a label often relieves them because it validates their struggle. As Dale Brown, one of our contributors, writes, "Learning about my problem changed me from a person who hated herself to someone who likes herself and knows that she is struggling with a real handicap."

And they do struggle. Each day must be negotiated emotionally, socially, and academically. As parents and teachers, we try to make it easier for them, but, in the end, they have to go through it by themselves.

The writings on these pages are evidence that these children are determined to survive anything that life throws at them. They do not place blame. They often acknowledge that they were not easy for their parents and teachers to handle—they are both challenged and challenging.

They talk of the compromises and the trade-offs. They talk of how they adjust to change and of their hopes, fears, and frustrations. They are sometimes confused by the mixed messages they receive. Parents and teachers may tell them they are smart, but their experiences often tell them they are not as successful academically as their classmates. Adults may tell them to try harder, yet they know they are trying as hard as they can.

You can see in their writings that they are often more open to challenge than we might expect. They are in the process of learning more about themselves, and their attitudes are evolving. They are asking for understanding and time to reach their potential. They want to be seen as different only in the sense that all people have differences. It is through understanding their differences that we and they can be open to their similarities and strengths.

It has been difficult for many of them to write about their problems. When they write, they must put a little of themselves on paper. They expose themselves to interpretation and misinterpretation. These are the voices not only of anger and frustration, but also of hope and expectation. Listen to them.

I Get Steamed

by Joseph Federico

I get steamed when I can't do anything I want to.

Joseph Federico drew this picture at age 6 as an assignment in his pre-kindergarten class. He dictated the caption to his teacher, Colleen Harrington. Joseph lives in Massachusetts.

Untitled

by F. Shea Weber

As lonely thoughts pass
Through my mind,

I can't sleep but,
I'm real sleepy,

I reach quietly for something,
I don't know what,
I'm sad, lonely and tired.

F. Shea Weber wrote this poem at age 9. His learning disability is in the area of writing. He has been in programs for the gifted since the first grade. He has attention deficit hyperactivity disorder, is disorganized, and, according to his mother, has a wonderful sense of humor. Shea lives in North Carolina.

Imprisoned Bug
by Sheri Miller

Small bug
    caught in a web
struggling to free yourself
from a prison of thread
        like us,
our life.

This poem originally appeared in the 1989 issue of Their World *magazine, a publication of the National Center for Learning Disabilities. Reprinted with permission.*

I Can

by Eli Jackson

I can.....

1. climb rocks

2. paddle a canoe

3. draw

4. paddle a kayak

5. play soccer

6. ski

7. hike

8. play archery

9. take care of animals

Eli Jackson penned this at age 10 while he was a fourth-grade student at Camperdown Academy. He wrote this to describe a few of his interests and strengths. He considers himself a naturalist who loves plants, animals, and the environment. Eli lives in South Carolina.

Misunderstood Child

by Jenifer Becker

Some of us reverse B's and D's

Some of us cannot read with ease

Perhaps our problem is with math

Or maybe it's a language path

But if you check our I.Q.'s

You will see that there are clues

That you should take great heed

Because we will succeed

Just take a look

In any history book

To see those of us you could not tame

To see those of us who have achieved great fame.

Jenifer Becker wrote this in the eighth grade as part of an English class assignment that asked the students to describe themselves. She lives in New York.

My Essay

by Chris Biner

I was born different from other people. My brain functions differently. I lose my temper a lot. I kick furniture when I am angry. I learn different. I open locks often. I listen to people and love reading. I have a hard time in science. I like division. I think it is easy. I feel proud of who I am.

I have lots of friends at school.

I want to be a truck trailer driver. So I could travel around the world. I need to finish school because it is important. I need to learn how to add up gas bills change flat tires turn on propane tanks and leave my place clean. In science I learned how to keep healthy.

By traveling with my mom I learned to get around roads. I also learned to read a map.

I do not like the fights that are going on in school. I wish they would stop because it makes me sad to see people get hurt. I wish people would be gentle.

The End

Chris Biner authored this at age 14 while he was a student in a severely handicapped/autistic program at a middle school. His skills are at a fifth- to eighth-grade level in all subjects except math. Chris lives in California.

The Great Dolphin

by Gavriel Kullman

Part 1

My name is Delphi Dolphin. I am a member of a pod which is really great, but I have a problem. My problem is that I can't keep up with the members of my pod. There is one good thing about being slow. I'm the only one who doesn't swim into nets. But the bad thing is I don't get to where the fish are fast enough, and if I don't start eating soon I will be a dead dolphin!

Sometimes we split up and decide to meet somewhere later and then I have the whole ocean to myself. That is when I go into my dream world. My dream world is a sparkling place, where all the slow dolphins of the world live. And they say, "We want to be just like you." Even though I know I'm dreaming it still makes me feel a lot better. I think "wow" someone looks up to "me." Why don't they look up to Zeus the elder dolphin. Then I had a very strange dream . . .

Part 2

In my dream I was swimming gracefully. I made a sharp turn and then I saw him. It was Zeus. Then I thought to myself "why would he be in my dream?" He started to swim my way so my first instinct was to swim away. Then I heard a voice. It sounded faint. It said, "Delphi why do you swim away from me?" "I swim away because I know I am in trouble," I said. The voice came again and then I knew it was him.

Then Zeus and I were talking. Then this thought came into my mind, "Why had he even come into my dream?" He said to me, "I have come to tell you something very important." Then I said, "What have you come to tell me?" "I am moving on and someone needs to lead the pod and I chose you," he said. I said, "Me? Why me? I don't even know the first thing about leading. How will I lead?" Then he said, "I will train you." Then we worked and worked and he taught me how to use my tail double time and use my sonar. Then he disappeared. He just vanished into thin water.

Part 3

When Zeus vanished, it amazed me. I thought, "Where is he?" I thought he was just pulling my fin, but he was really gone. After he vanished I found myself in the real ocean. I went to go find the pod and then out of nowhere, there they were. I wanted to show them all the stuff that Zeus had taught me and I did, but no one paid attention. Then I went back to try to find Zeus and then he appeared. He said, "Delphi, I have been watching you as you have been trying to convince them. You can't try. You have to make them know." So then with Zeus's words in my head I went out and lived by myself (for at least 4 or 5 hours). And then they said that I was getting more fish than them. And then as time went on I led the great pod. And now it is my turn to move on and then pick someone else.

Gavriel Kullman wrote this as a class assignment at age 12. He has been diagnosed with dyslexia and attention deficit disorder without hyperactivity. He attends public school in California.

Testing Day at Jemicy

by Caitlin McCormick

The silence, the fear of what's ahead,
slowly slowly,
Taking your time to wind your way to the room,
slowly slowly
The room you dread most,
slowly slowly
There she waits with the tests,
The dreaded test in front of her,
slowly slowly
The tests you soon will be taking,
slowly slowly
You approach the door,
slowly slowly
You swing the door wide open,
slowly slowly,
You walk down the hall,
slowly slowly,
You see her door,
slowly slowly,
You open it
slowly slowly,
There she waits,
slowly slowly

*Caitlin McCormick wrote this at age 11 while attending the Jemicy School.
She lives in Maryland.*

Dyslexia

by Julie Blanchard

when I found out I had dyslexia
I was surprised and wanted to know
everything about it. When I found out what
it was I wanted to tell everyone but I was not to tell
any one because they did not want people to make frown
of me so I only told my best friends I know right then me
and my brother both had dyslexia he and I whir the only
people in are family and I was happy to know that sum
one else had it. A couple day lhter I founed out I had A
atanshandafasit I ast what that was to and from than on I
have ben taking medasin for it. Sum times I whnder am I
spashal do I have a gift whay did god chows me did I Just
hapin to be fit for this part but I do know I have a gift
and sum day I will know what it is but I have ben the
sam person aver shans I have ben bourn.

When I found out I had dyslexia I was surprised and
wanted to know everything about it. When I found out what it
was I wanted to tell everyone but I was not to tell anyone
because they did not want people to make fun of me, so I only
told my best friends I knew right then. Me and my brother
both had dyslexia. He and I were the only people in our family
and I was happy to know that someone else had it. A couple of
days later I found out I had an attention deficit. I asked what

that was too, and from then on I have been taking medicine for it. Sometimes I wonder: Am I special? Do I have a gift? Why did God choose me? Did I just happen to fit this part? But I do know I have a gift and someday I will know what it is, but I have been the same person ever since I have been born.

Julie Blanchard wrote the first piece when she was 11 years old and a student at Landmark School. The second piece is the edited version. Both originally appeared in the Spring 1994 issue of Gazette, *published by the Learning Disabilities Association of Massachusetts.*

My Learning Disability

by Thomas Lennon

Dyslexia is not a disease. It's just a learning problem. It doesn't have to overcome you; you have to overcome it. When people have dyslexia, they can have a serious learning problem or a minor learning problem. My problem is remembering things I hear. But I can remember for days, the things I see. I also have trouble paying attention in class. When I was in my old school I used to look outside and look at the cars drive by.

Anyone that's black or white or any religion can get it. You're actually born with it. People don't know how we can get it. It just happens to us. There are many ways you can get it, one of them is when your parents have dyslexia . . .

It can affect you and your parents by many things. You have problems with one, two or even four subjects. When I was twelve months old my parents did a test to finish a fifteen piece puzzle and I finished it in ten minutes. My parents thought one time I was deaf when I was one or two years old but when my mom opened the cookie jar I started running for a cookie. So you can see that we're not dumb but we're smart, but we're weak in some places . . .

Thomas Lennon was a 14-year-old student at the Carroll School when he wrote the above. He was the recipient of the 1994 Coach's Award for sportsmanship and athletic achievement.

WHY

by Richard Brodeur

Why is a term used to want to know something

Fight is a struggle to get something

Education is the knowledge, skill, ability or

Character developed by teaching in a method

Suitable to the learner.

Need is something a person has to have to survive

Suitable is something that works

Then why is it so hard to get a suitable

Method of teaching in our public schools

And why do people have to suffer in school . . .

I wish I could answer the **Why** for you and

For me—but I can not.

Richard Brodeur wrote this at age 13 after a tutor finally showed him that he could learn and that his difficulties were not a result of an emotional disorder but of an auditory processing problem. A student at Landmark School, he has been elected to the student council and has won many awards for outstanding academic achievement in math, science, and history. His future plans include playing basketball and going to college to major in political science or law. He lives in New York.

A Letter from a Learning Disabled Child

by Michael Fleischer

Hello, my name is Michael Fleischer. I have a learning disability. I am twelve years old and in the 7th grade. . . . I am in all accelerated classes and at the end of the first term, I made High Honors, all A's. The reason I am writing this essay is to let people and other kids who have learning disabilities know that this problem does not mean you are dumb or unable to participate and compete in activities as well as kids without learning disabilities. It just means you have to try harder.

I was diagnosed as severe to profoundly deaf shortly after I was born. I went to the deaf school to learn sign language as an infant. Something happened and Children's Hospital discovered I could hear but I wasn't talking. I went to a special school at Children's Hospital to learn to talk for two years. I also have private speech therapy. As I grew up, I learned I had an auditory processing problem. That means I have trouble learning by listening. I need school work written down on the blackboard. I also have some attention deficit problems which means I have problems focusing and paying attention in class for long periods of time. I also have some motor (and visual-motor) coordinating problems which makes handwriting hard and tiring. I can't listen and write at the same time. I have problems in sequencing, and identifying the main ideas in stories, and picking out the important things to study from the unimportant details. I hate book reports but I do them. I also can drive my parents crazy with my tactile sensitivity. I never wear my socks right. I always turn them inside out because the seams bother me as do other clothes. All that this means is that I need extra help to accomplish what I want to do. I have been going to a Special Ed tutor after school twice a week for the last couple of years and also have received Occupational Therapy and Sensory Integration Therapy. I also have a special friend, Dr. Kristine S., who tests me each year to help the school know how to support me. My school teachers are great and have helped me after school, but my biggest supporters and helpers have been my parents. All this extra help takes a lot of time out of my social life but it is well worth it. (Though at the beginning I didn't think so.)

I like sports and have been on the Little League baseball team, the Swim team, Soccer team and Tennis team. I recently won the 7th grade singles tennis championship for middle school. I have a lot of friends and when time is available we get together and play football, basketball and street hockey. I like to collect baseball cards and stamps and in the past have even auditioned and danced in the ballet, The Nutcracker Suite, at the Walnut Hill School for Performing Arts. I never had ballet lessons (and I never want to) but I just wanted to perform and it sounded like fun. It was.

Last year, I performed at Faneuil Hall when I played the clarinet as the youngest member of the MetroWest Community Band. This year I joined the MetroWest Youth Symphony Orchestra and our next concert is with the New England Philharmonics. I play 1st clarinet in both my school band and school orchestra and this winter I am going to try out for the Massachusetts Northeastern Junior All-District Band. I think I will make it. But if I don't make it, I will just practice harder than ever so I will be sure to make it the next year. There is a poster in my vice-principal's office that says "You only fail, when you stop trying." If you keep trying you can't fail.

I am Michael Fleischer. A normal kid. I like music and sports and enjoy my friends like other normal kids. But there isn't any such thing as a "normal" kid really. Everyone has special traits and talents and everyone learns in a different way. Yes, it does take me longer to get my homework done and

I need to study harder than some of my friends but having a learning disability has never held me back. It never will. You just have to try harder and keep trying and you can succeed.

Michael Fleischer's letter originally appeared in the Winter 1994 Gazette, published by the Learning Disabilities Association of Massachusetts. It is reprinted here with his and his mother's permission. They live in Massachusetts.

Dyslexia

by Virginia Wise

I'm dyslexic which is not fun to be,

I have to live with it because it's part of me.

Sometimes you get bothered by it,

but I know what to do,

just call Carroll teachers and they will help you.

When it eats you inside,

and you really want to hide.

It's maddening,

It's saddening,

but that's the way it's got to be,

because it's part of me!

Virginia Wise composed this at age 12 while she was a student at the Carroll School. She has a learning disability that affects her reading. She enjoys art. Virginia Wise is from Massachusetts.

Speech Given to the School Board

by Jeremy Smith

I'm Jeremy Smith. I'm 12 years old and in the 5th grade. I also belong to the Screen Actors Guild and am a member of the American Federation of Television and Radio Artists.

I have delayed bone growth and Attention Deficit Disorder. I also have a processing problem and a fine motor delay which makes it hard for me to write. I have been in the Resource Specialists Program (RSP) since I was in first grade.

Now I only go to RSP one hour a week. I get good grades and I really like going to school. My RSP teacher helps me by catching me up on work if it's hard for me. She helps my classroom teachers understand my problems so they don't think I'm stupid or have a bad attitude.

Kids used to tease me about my size and my handwriting, but my RSP teacher helped me by telling me it doesn't matter what they think, it's what I think of myself that counts.

If I didn't have RSP I think I wouldn't be doing as well. I'm thankful to the people who understand my problems and the way they handled it. I think every kid with a disability needs special understanding because it's not easy to be different. Some kids might think they are stupid or bad if they don't know they have a disability and get the help and understanding they need.

My sister says: I'm not disabled, the system is disabled because God made everyone different . . . and I believe her.

Jeremy Smith made this presentation to his school board as part of a community request for more sensitivity on the part of teachers and better enforcement of Section 504 of the Rehabilitation Act of 1973, which prohibits any agency receiving federal funds from discriminating against a person because of a disability. He lives in California.

Me

by Emily Gross

I am like a crystal prism,
With many different sides to me,
I can only achieve my rainbow,
When someone helps to provide me the light.

I sometimes feel as though I
have been put in a dark room,
Where light is a privilege that must be earned instead of a
right.
And where my rainbow is not always welcome.

Then sometimes, I feel the world is a blank page,
And I am there to spread my colors across it.

There are times when my rainbow stretches halfway,
And someone else's meets mine in the middle,
And both our rainbows come together to form
A pot of gold called friendship.

I hope that one day the whole world
Will create one big cauldron
Of gold,
And everyone together,
Will share the wealth.

This poem was originally published in the 1993 issue of Their World *magazine and is reprinted with permission. Emily Gross wrote this at age 13 as an English assignment, explaining to her mother that "Mr. F. wanted us to write about ourselves, but I didn't want to tell him ANYTHING about me, so I used a metaphor!"*

WORK

by Michael Sapienza

Teachers can make you WORK.

Parents can make you WORK.

Friends can make you WORK.

But the only way things will ever

WORK is if YOU WORK!

WORK you have to WORK to make

things WORK.

Michael Sapienza authored this poem at age 13 while he was a student at the Carroll School. He is a talented actor who has for two years held the lead role in "Arts Night," his school's annual performance by the art department. He lives in Massachusetts.

Last

by Tara Cashin

Last, Last, Last

Never first—always last

I sit so still

and so quiet but

Still Last, Last

Last

Tara Cashin was an 11-year-old student at the Crossroads School when she wrote this. She lives in Pennsylvania.

From Behind Closed Doors

by Matthew Payne

Since I have been going to Oakland, it has changed me in so many ways, in the way I act, feel and make friends.

Before I came here I was bored, miserable, and got into a lot of trouble at my old school. Kids would beat up on me if I didn't do what they wanted or give them what they wanted. I would find myself being teased when my friends were in 3rd, 4th and 5th grades. I was disliked by all of my classmates, except for one. His name is John and he seemed normal but for one thing: he was deaf. I told my parents everything, yet they did nothing. I was failing. My teachers acted as though they did not even like me. I would receive in-school suspension and in-house suspension. I was mad!

Then one day my parents realized what was going on with me. They began looking around for a new school for me to go to. It took months. All those months it took them to find a school I was at home, feeling sorry for myself, ashamed, and sometimes even hating myself. On some nights, I could hear my whole family downstairs fighting, and that scared me so much.

One day my mom was talking to a friend at church about my problem, and the woman mentioned that she had sent her son Daniel to a place called Oakland. So one day we rode to this school, and it seemed okay. I was enrolled for the following summer, and that arrived very fast.

I was nervous and didn't want to come. I was scared of being threatened or even beaten up. When I got there, I would not even get out of the car. I was crying and fighting my parents.

Then, while I was sitting in the car, a person walked up to me named Peter. He looked a little weird to me at first, but he was nice. Once I got out of the car he took me around to meet other students. . . . I got to know some kids my age, and they got along with me!

When school started I also noticed that the rooms were different. They were clean—no graffiti on the walls—and there wasn't anyone waiting to beat you up as you walked in. The teachers were nice and cared, and everything was organized. The classes were small, compared to having almost 40 kids in a class.

The school changed me. I am passing, having fun, and even making friends. It's been a year and a half, and I have lots of friends now. Not only that, but I have overcome my fears and feel good about myself. I have friends I will never forget.

All I can say is that I'm glad that I got out of the car. I have something now I thought I would never have.

Matthew Payne was 16 years old and a student at the Oakland School when he wrote this essay. He has attention deficit disorder. He lives in Virginia.

What's on the Inside

by Mike Uhrich

Inside of me
there is creativity
running through my body like a river,
flowing into a lake.
Inside of me
is a purring cat
happy to be petted,
playful and curious.
Inside of me
is a castle on a hill
surrounded by trees.
Sometimes at war with an army of knights,
sometimes in peace with the enemy.
Inside of me
a tree grows unharmed,
branches reaching out as far as they can,
roots growing down to good soil.
Inside of me
a key waits
for someone to unlock the chest
and free the treasure.

Mike Uhrich wrote this at age 13. At age 7 he was diagnosed with attention deficit hyperactivity disorder and learning disabilities. He lives in Washington.

What You Need to Have to Be Dyslexic

by Anson McNulty

Life for Dyslexic kids can be hard, especially if you don't have a lot of determination, hope, curiosity, and a strong desire to learn.

The reason why you need **determination** is because you can't ever give up. For example, if you were in a room with five different doors and they all have five different signs on top, you cannot give up until you find the right door to let you out. Also, you need determination because life won't be as simple for you as it is for other people. You will learn to read, but you won't have as easy a time as your friends who are not dyslexic. But the most important thing is that you always learn whatever you set your goal on. No matter what it is, determination will help get you there.

You will need **hope** if you are a dyslexic. Most hope that they will learn how to read, write and spell so that they can make it in the world on their own. But they also hope to overcome it in their own way because they must be able to depend on themselves for answers. Finally, you must have hope that you won't ever give up because that is the greatest temptation of all. In the beginning you always do things wrong in your language skills, and it makes you not want to try to do all those things over and over until you finally get some of them right. Hope will give you something to go on learning for.

Curiosity makes your learning easier. You must have curiosity to do all sorts of subjects in school. For instance, if you want knowledge about the Greeks, curiosity is the first step. It makes it easier to learn new things if you have a lot of questions that you would like to know the answers to. But curiosity is also about wanting to do new things, like playing a new sport, too. If you are dyslexic you must have a good subject or skill to fall back on when you need support. Curiosity helps you find that special thing you have a talent for.

You must have a **desire for learning** to be able to persevere the hard times that you will most definitely go through if you are dyslexic or have a very similar learning disability such as A.D.D. You can make it work if you try your hardest to read and write, but it may be very, very difficult to attain. Being dyslexic makes it hard to find out interesting information when you are not in school because you cannot just pick up a *National Geographic* magazine and learn interesting facts about the world, especially animals. You must ask someone to read you the story or article which after a while becomes very stressful to some people. Although you can wait for later to read the book and turn on your TV set to get information, most dyslexics would like to read a book. It makes me mad when I see my friends who can read, sit and watch T.V. when I have to work and work to be able to read on my own.

So, if you have determination, curiosity, hope, and the desire to learn, you will have a much easier life, even if you aren't dyslexic. If you are dyslexic, you must have these qualities to overcome the obstacles to learning.

Anson McNulty is a 14-year-old student at the Kildonan School. This essay was originally published in the school's journal of creative writing, The Kaleidoscope, *in June 1994. Anson describes functioning with dyslexia as living "like a bat without radar." He lives in New York.*

Untitled

by Larry Volk

am I enough

to fill the dreams of my parents

have I been enough

for them to be proud of

is the smiling child of youth

growing upright

I tried so hard

I was the one who didn't know when to stop

I was the one with the flowers

I carried a smile outside and a frown inside

always working for praise

but finding more mischief

the one with the problem

I hope I'm enough

I have given of myself

finally I am being myself

we don't agree on everything

and I'm still learning

maybe it's just me

what if what I dream

is not their dream

what if my joy

is not theirs

I want them to be proud

I need their love

I need their support

are they proud of my dream

of my life

of . . . me

This poem was first published in the 1983 issue of Their World *magazine, published by the National Center for Learning Disabilities, and is reprinted with permission.*

COURAGE: Fighting My Fears

by Jeffrey Proctor

I don't recall much about the fifth grade, but I can remember just a few main aspects that I'll never forget. I began my fifth grade school term with a great deal of difficulty. My learning disabilities included hardships taking down notes and recording everything that the teacher put down on that big green blackboard, which seemed to tower over me like a huge monster, taunting and laughing with evil delight at my troubles.

At first these notes were easy. Then they began to increase in amount, and soon my vision turned blurry. The notes changed into nothing but one big collage of scribbles and diagrams. Worksheets and other assignments were just like this. The teacher, who we'll call Mr. Worme (for security reasons), gave the class one page of mathematical problems, each page jammed with work that I wasn't exactly sure I could finish. To my fears, I was right. I found myself still working while the students around me were finished. It's very difficult to explain the situation I was in; I felt surrounded, and very uncomfortable. At times, I'd often glance around to see if anyone was looking at me and notice that I was the slowest kid in the whole room. I'd have to turn in my assignments incomplete. Each day I would do the same thing, and hope dearly that the teacher didn't ask why it wasn't finished on time.

Soon this problem became worse. I went to my parents, who developed a plan to sign my homework at a certain point if I didn't finish enough in time. I had a terrible fear that Mr. Worme wouldn't accept this, and I'd get in trouble. With tears rolling down my cheeks I seriously begged my parents not to do this. Later, my parents' plan worked, but I couldn't stand the chance that the teacher would ask me in front of the whole class and expose my problems. (He was that kind of person.)

By not completing my work in time, I was subject to several different situations. First, I'd have to stay in for recess and finish the work. Second, Mr. Worme would call my parents and discuss the matter, which would result in another discussion once I got home. Finally, third and probably the most dreadful of them all, the class would take notice of my slowness, the teacher would ask me about it in front of everyone, and I'd either get situation A or B. The key to all this was embarrassment and fear, something I could never deal with, and something that would carry on all the way into the seventh grade.

The seventh grade was a whole new ballgame. Once passing through that big spiked bridge I was attacked with new methods and forceful educational tactics. I found this to be the most difficult grade yet, and I was forced to make new choices and commitments that would affect my education.

Out of all my classes, History and Pre-Algebra turned out to be the hardest encounters. Both teachers cared little about my problems, and maintained a bullyish behavior, stating that not keeping up was my problem. Eventually, every problem that I had in the fifth grade came back as a flashback in the form of a Mack truck. Note taking gave me the same difficulty, but with only double the amount. They gave me large quantities of assignments as well. History included roughly three pages with twenty-five problems on each sheet. Algebra, the only alien language in the form of English language, was packed with book pages whose concepts I didn't understand.

The embarrassment also returned. I had the same fear of exposing my problems to the rest of the class. I never really had the courage to confront the teacher and confess my problems, add the details, and ask for a solution to better help my needs. This added a very heavy burden on my life while in the seventh grade. Soon after pre-algebra turned so difficult that I was transferred to a basic math class, but unfortunately I remained trapped in History. By the end of the year I knew I would be going to my next school the following year in Springfield, Massachusetts, a school specially designed for students with my problems and others like them. I was disappointed to leave my friends behind, but I'd also be leaving the hell I had to put up with in algebra and history. The next year in my new school would be the best experience of my life.

Today, thanks to special programs and schools like mine, I'm better able to adapt to situations such as those I faced. I am less embarrassed when facing the teacher, and when I have a problem, I know that I'm not afraid to tell someone. For other students out there, I can only say this: If there's one thing that a student with learning disabilities must do, it's to have the courage to ask questions in front of the class, and to have the strength to do it. If you have a problem you can't get in trouble for it. Teachers are supposed to help one way or another, and you're supposed to ask for that help. I was so embarrassed to ask for help that I would wait until after school to do it, away from other students. If the teacher doesn't realize what's going on, he/she will never know, and you'll be caught in a great many hardships. I should know—I did the same.

Jeffrey Proctor wrote this at age 14 while he was attending the White Oak School. He lives in Massachusetts.

Untitled

by Nick Stead

I remember the day like it was yesterday. My mother and I were at a stop sign on Main Street. I was only five, sitting in the back seat of a tan Cadillac, restless as usual. My mother turned around and said, "Nick!" Her voice cracked; I still don't know if she was going to cry or if her voice was sore from yelling at me for playing with the seatbelt. She continued, "Your dad and I and all your teachers think that you should stay back."

"Mom, but all my friends are going to first grade."

"Nick, maybe one of your friends might stay back, too."

"Who, Mom?"

"Joe."

Gullible old me said, "OK," and thought nothing of it for the rest of the summer.

When I started school the next year, Joe wasn't in school. I didn't know anybody, but staying back wasn't so bad after all. No one made fun of me that year because I was bigger than them.

Now nine years later I still get teased about staying back in kindergarten, but now I just say, "Ya, I couldn't stack the blocks as high as the other kids."

When Nick Stead wrote this at age 14, he was a student at the Carroll School. At Carroll he received the 1994 Wings of Glory and Citizenship awards: for athletic performance and good citizenship in school. He lives in Massachusetts.

Mommy

by Heather Hauri

When I was little,
I would make messes,
And even rip my dresses;

Fall down on the ground
And scrape my knee,
Mommy would fix it,
And say she loved me.

Sneaky as a cat,
Sly as a rat,
Being a brat,
Acting like that—

Running too fast,
Slip in the mud,
Fall on my butt with a thud,
Then Mom helped me up,
Cause she was my bud.

Ice cream on my nose,
Wiggly little toes,
Trying on clothes
With a little kid pose,
Mommy would laugh,
Because she knew for sure,
That I loved her.

Stay up all night,
She'd tuck me in tight,
Blow me a kiss,
And turn off the light.

Wake-up in the morn,
And crawl in Mom's bed,
She'd kiss me on the head,
And sometimes she said,
"It's too early go back to sleep"
If I couldn't I'd count sheep,
It was plain to see,
That I loved her & she loved me.

Later on that day
We'd go outside & play,
Me and Mom walking side by side—
We went to the park,
And swung on the swings,
I just loved doing those things.
I looked up to her,
She looked down then I could see,
She did love me!

Heather Hauri is a seventh-grade middle school student who has been diagnosed with attention deficit hyperactivity disorder. She wrote this poem as part of a "Write on" program for special children. Her mother, Joanne Harris, has written a poem to her daughter, which appears in chapter 5, "Family Voices." Heather and her mother live in California.

Untitled

by Amy Epstein

I can feel the warm spring breeze on my face. "I wish I were outside playing," I say to myself. I could be practicing soccer or playing with my friends, but no, I am stuck going to the children's hospital on a perfectly good Saturday morning!

All my life things have not come easily for me . . . spelling, remembering and even copying. I am in third grade, and especially now, I am noticing this. I remember my mom's explanation, "Now your teachers will have a reason for your problems, and they will know you are not making it up. Instead of being frustrated with you, they will know how to help you." Yes, sir, my parents have always had the best faith in me. They have supported me the whole time.

My mom was not that far off when she said I was frustrating teachers. I think I drove most of my teachers crazy, and the ones that I didn't, I made a serious crack in their sanity. I have trouble learning the basics, but once I learn the basics, I have no trouble grasping onto concepts.

I remember the Thursday nights, "Spelling Test Studying." Yes that was the worst. I could never seem to get it right. It was so frustrating. Even more so, if that could be, were the multiplication facts. I could not tell you how many times I almost gave up and decided to become a bum. Again my parents pushed and pushed. I remember one time we were eating dinner, and my dad said, "Amy, what is 4x3?" I would answer, "24?" Then my parents would say, "Well, we will have to work on that." Anyway now I am off to the hospital to have testing done. I am a little upset, because all my life I have been trying to become just like all the other kids, and this is just bringing me further away from being a normal kid. I am glad, however, because now I do have an explanation, and sometimes that is worth the small amount of temperamental unhappiness.

We got the test results back about a week later. We found out that I have a significant learning disability. My mom gave a copy to all my teachers. This was not the end, however. This is only the beginning.

The frustrations of my life are still very much with me. I am still made fun of when I misspell "easy" words. I still feel bad, but if the person teasing me can't understand my problem, they are the ones to blame, not me. I have learned to cope with my problems, and I just hope that someday kids like me will be more accepted in life!

Amy Epstein wrote this in 1990 when she was an eighth grader at the Cohen Hillel Academy in Swampscott, Massachusetts.

The Sobbing Cry

by Carvell Estriplet

The sobbing cry

of a reading eye

no human can deny.

There lies someone near

that I used to fear

being lost, and confused,

that cost a lot,

I could not lie,

I was too shy

I felt like to die.

That's why the fight

that brought me into the sight

of the Principal's eye.

Those days brought me into a phase,

and then a daze. That's why I faded into a shade

I look very mad, but I was very sad.

That's why I lost every

thing except my pride.

I faced the odds,

I tried real hard,

but just get a grade like the

letter that started in 'frog.'

It got better in a split second light, then

I was on the sight, of new school, and my

dreams got brighter, so did my mind.

Carvell Estriplet wrote this when he was 15 years old and a student at the Carroll School. While there, he received the 1994 Coach's Award for achievement in athletics. His learning disability is in reading. He is now in high school. Carvell Estriplet lives in Massachusetts.

The Gifted LD Child

Author unknown

I wonder who decided that smart guys
Have got to make A's?
I wonder why school athletes
Always get all the praise?
I wonder what kind of society
Would make the stupid rule,
That if you can't compete with others.
You must be a useless fool.
Even when I work hard at school,
It seems I'm always behind.
The kids either ignore me,
Or are cruel and unkind.
Teacher, I wish you would notice me,
I can't learn like the rest.
But if you'll find a way to teach me,
I promise I'll do my best.
I have trouble learning phonics.
Short E and I sound alike.
Guess I'll go home and repair
My broken minibike.
When I read, I always lose my place.
The words get all jumbled up.
Last Saturday I showed my horse,
And won a silver trophy cup.
Social Studies isn't much fun.

Reading about China is boring.
Wish I could read about Robbers' Cave
Where my family went exploring.
My fingers won't write test answers,
Even when they're in my head.
Why can't I just tell you, teacher,
Or use the typewriter, instead?
I never can catch or throw a ball,
Coach, I'm the clumsiest guy around,
But I got two coons the other night,
Just me and my old hound.
How will I ever get any better,
If no one has the time to teach?
If I sit on the sidelines all my life,
What goals will I ever reach?
I can't keep up with kids in class,
Don't compare me to my brothers,
Just give me a chance to grow at my pace,
Without competing with the others.
Wish someone would try to teach me,
Though I can't learn like the rest.
If someone cared enough to reach me,
I promise, I'd really do my best.

This poem originally appeared in the 1983 issue of Their World *magazine of the National Center for Learning Disabilities and is reprinted with permission.*

It's Not an Excuse!

by Scott M. Martin

David has a learning disability
Yellow buses give him nightmares
School is against him
Learning to hate life
Eager to get out
Xed out of society
Innocence turning
Coming to insanity

David is now very Frustrated
Yearning for help
Some one any one
Living in a hell
Elevator stuck in the basement
XI is not some thing to learn
In and out of schools
Abvdefhgopijklmnopqrstucvwxyz

Scott M. Martin wrote this while attending the Kildonan School, where he was vice president of the student council. He states, "As I progress in life I show the people who thought I was going to fail just the opposite. Some people may say you cannot always succeed, but a failure at one point in time can be good because you can learn from that and grow even more." He lives in New Jersey.

Untitled

by Timothy DeMars

My learning disability shows up everywhere in my life, not just in school. One incident was when I was at the fruit market. I grabbed a handful of cherries. My mother told my sister to get a plastic bag from the roll. My sister had a difficult time opening the bag. Instead of concentrating on the cherries I tried to help her. The cherries started falling out of my hand. Then the owner started to yell at me saying I was dropping the cherries on the floor and I was making a mess. I felt angry and embarrassed. My mom understood what happened and said the guy thought I was a regular kid acting stupid. It is harder for me to cope with my disability when these things happen.

When Timothy DeMars wrote this, he was a 13-year-old student at the White Oak School. He has attention deficit disorder. He plays the piano and hopes to become a meteorologist. He lives in Massachusetts.

Sidewalk; "Riffs Begin on Words"
by Chris Hines

Bob Jones, is blind to the way of life
That is the way to be
"Can't you see," he says, "don't be me, be you."
"Who?"
People trapped within themselves forgotten realms
Their lives guided by broken helms of hope.
Can't be found can't you hear the sound
Of the silent scream.
You know what it means?
We're free, saved from the blindness.

South takes over this time
an army of climbing mimes with hope,
that the clear wall doesn't fall
into your mind behind an iron curtain.
But they know they left guilt about a mile ahead.

Algebra, yeah ain't no fun, for everyone
But hey, they say I'm dyslexic, hey I'm not everyone!
Take me out of class, break the glass, let me walk
without harass
-ment. People are so stressed out, can't let it out
So why don't you pour it on me, maybe not.

Chris Hines wrote this at 16 while he was attending the Kildonan School. It was originally printed in the school's journal of creative writing, The Kaleidoscope, *in spring 1994. Chris describes being dyslexic as "having a flashlight in a dark basement and not being able to find the battery for it." He lives in Virginia.*

Some Thoughts on Learning Disabilities

Author unknown

Yes, I'm in a special class. Being in a special class is hard to deal with. Most of my classmates can be behavior problems, but I see why. It is frustrating when you can't read and you have people laughing at you because of this. Hey look world, I didn't ask to have a learning disability. I know it's frustrating but some of us have learned to control ourselves. Most of the people in my classes are the smartest people I know but their disability makes it such that they seem dumb.

I've been in a special class since the third grade. I have what they call dyslexia. I didn't even know what the word meant. When I try to read the words get real blurry. They jump up and down on the page and usually I end up with a headache. I know I'm smart but I just don't have the tools to show it. It is a disability that is very embarrassing and I wish people would understand it and me.

I feel different and I'm treated differently. People laugh because I need extra help—some even call me retarded! I know I'm not but I am special. When I sit down to complete a 10 minute homework assignment it can take me up to an hour to do. I'll make it and I'm sure my future will be more promising than some of the ones that laugh at me now!

If you have a disability, I would like to tell you that the road ahead is not easy—but we'll make it. To sum it all up—don't quit, no matter what!!!

This essay was written by a ninth-grade student with learning disabilities. It was published in the fall 1990 issue of Exceptional Parent, *a journal of the Council for Exceptional Children. It is reprinted with permission.*

Out with the D a m Frustration
by Matthew Mills

I never thought I would make the journey
It was like trying to fall upward out of a tree
the days were long the work
was as hard as reading Chinese

I ask for no pity
just some one to know what it is like
to go through this journey
like a blind man driving
I struggle to stay between the lines.

there are many that can't
complete the expedition
that is as long as a life time

to get the help for this incorrigibility
or other wise lazy is like moving a
wheel barrow with a square wheel

But the word is out

the word is d a m

the word is frustration

the journey

will

never

e

n

d

Matthew Mills wrote this at age 17 while he was a student at the Kildonan School. He was president of the student council at Kildonan. He feels his biggest achievement in life has been overcoming the challenge of dyslexia. He lives in Maryland.

Harness

by Dale Brown

I forged a metal harness
made of heavy chain.
Despite severe discomfort
I placed it on my brain.
I seemed to be unable
though I searched hard to find,
Another method to control
my overactive mind.
My brain, it groaned and whimpered,
trembled, moaned and plead.
Before it had been free,
not trapped inside my head.
Free—yes, free to wander,
to dance in sparkling sun.
Not using freedom wisely,
it had a lot of fun.
It daydreamed and it fiddled
with its pictures and its words.
Equations and experiments,
it mashed and minced and stirred.
As much as I enjoyed
just letting my brain go,
unless it learned some discipline,
it would never grow.
For full of bubbling ideas
as a brain may be,
it must learn to make its dreams
become reality.
So I placed the harness
around my bucking brain,

hoping hard that it would try
to endure the strain.
Instead it wormed and wiggled
in an attempt to glide
or slip out of the harness
which it was trapped inside.
I pulled the harness tight
to hold my brain within
I was fighting with my brain,
and I was going to win.
My brain began to tremble,
quiver, quake, and shout,
"I hurt. I hate this harness.
Please! Oh let me out."
"Oh no," I angrily replied.
"You've caused me enough pain.
Inside my lovely harness
you simply must remain."
But with a very final
and disdainful jerk,
my brain blew up my harness
and all my sweaty work.
To my left's a broken harness.
To my right lies links of chain.
But someday, I'll find a way
to capture me my brain.

Dale Brown started writing this poem when she was 14. She worked on it for three years and finished it when she graduated from high school. More of her poetry can be found in her book, I Know I Can Climb the Mountain *(Mountain Books). Dale Brown lives in Washington, D.C.*

There Is More to Life Than a Learning Disability

by Karen Klein

I used to think that if you are diagnosed with the case of "Learning Disability" then you are a domby. Well, I don't think that any more. I think that there is more to life than having a "Learning Disability" problem. I had a rough life, but it makes me stronger by letting everything soak in my brain. We have a lot to discover about the case of "Learning Habits." I have a lot in my brain already, but I have a whole life in front of me to discover yet!!! . . . You have to get people to listen. You never give up all your dreams just because of it. You make a lot of changes. If you think about it, having a learning problem is not so bad. Some of the times you just think that you are like one of the guys.

Karen Klein authored this when she was in high school. It originally appeared in the 1992 issue of Their World *magazine of the National Center for Learning Disabilities and is reprinted with permission.*

The Fear Within Me—A Real Life Horror Story

by Catharine Grace

Cast of Characters
Catharine E. Grace as herself
Mrs. H—5th grade math teacher
Featuring: the blackboard
Extras—the rest of Catharine's classmates

Scene 1

Outside the sun shines with a yellow, golden brightness that engulfs the playground and school. I can distinctly hear the birds chirping in the early April morning light. The chirping sounds almost magnified, completely drowning out the sound of Mrs. H.'s demanding, bellowing voice explaining new equations.

What on earth could she be talking about now? My ten-year-old mind honestly doesn't care. I'd rather listen to the birds chirping or gaze at the butterfly that proceeds to flutter profusely around and around the window pane.

In the classroom there is this impending darkness surrounding me. I feel totally lost. In intense horror I lose myself staring at Mrs. H.'s double chin, buddha-styled face and brown piercing, beady eyes. Oh God, I see that gleam in her eyes. She's getting ready to call on us, on me especially. She's out to get me.

I avert my eyes from her direction and I burn them through the page of the math book—page 109, fractions. For some absurd, unknown reason, I figure if I stare at the page full of problems more and more, the better of an understanding I will have, when in reality, I only get more confused. To

me, examining a page of fractions is like trying to follow
directions on a road map being held upside down.

In desperation I wonder if I can fake a sudden illness. My
stomach is hurting me. To be honest, my stomach always feels
like it is going to cave in when Mrs. H. writes out the long,
never-ending fractions on the board for her pupils to solve, or
at least make an attempt to solve.

At this point my heart is making this very loud, clear,
abrupt, thumpity-thump noise. I can feel its beat pounding in
and out of my sweater. "Oh God, please don't let Mrs. H. call
on me," I silently pray. During these times I can grow into a
very religious child, though I normally don't like going to
church every Sunday. If there is a God, then, "God, don't let
her pick me. Okay? PLEASE? I promise from this point on to be
good. I even promise to put in fifty cents instead of the measly
twenty-five cents I usually throw into collection."

With wide, fearful, blue-green eyes, I witness Mrs. H.
picking out classmates sitting around me to approach the
intimidating blackboard and solve the problem. I sit and
watch her extend her arm with its rolls of fat and her chubby,
red dragon-painted fingers pointing in an erratic fashion. With
the sweat pouring from my palms and forehead, I could grease
a cookie sheet instead of using Crisco. I feel my body tremble.
A nervous twitch starts in my right eye. Maybe I do have an
illness. Maybe I can make a run for the door. Oh God, don't let
the big old bag call on me.

"I'll get you and your little pesty dog too!" The wicked
witch! I bet Mrs. H., when a child, idolized the Wicked Witch
of the west and despised Dorothy.

I hear her praising students who followed every step
correctly in the way she wanted it done. I see the students
returning to their seats with triumphant looks splashed across
their faces. All I want to do is reach out and hit them. Why
can't I be like those kids? "The other kids," is how I refer to the
smarties when I explain my woes and disappointments to my

mom day after day. "Mom, why can't I be as smart as they are?"

Some of the kids are even willingly raising their hands. They, the few, the smart, the brave know-it-alls, actually <u>want</u> to go to the board because they know the answer. That's what I, with extreme envy, think to myself.

Okay, I've gone this far with Mrs. H. not calling me. Maybe this could be my lucky day. I feel my spirits soar. "Cathy Grace, do number 12 please." The rest is history. The same song and dance. I can't remember the steps. I stare at the book, number 12. I look at the blackboard. I then look at the piece of big, yellow chalk. I feel the twenty-five pairs of eyes staring at me. I hear some students tapping their feet or pencils. I look at the clock. Class is almost over, only three more stupid minutes. Maybe the witch will let me go, forget about the problem.

For the sake of writing something down, I write blah, blah, blah, whatever. I stare with great hopelessness at Mrs. H. My eyes are silently whispering, whimpering, pleading, "Help me." Mrs. H. pushes up her rolls of fat and waddles over to assist me. "This is all wrong," she unmercifully announces. With her flabby arm, she erases the whole problem and proceeds to complete it herself.

It is recess time and all the kids are waiting for Mrs. H. to hurry up, finish my problem, and shut up and let them go out and play with their other friends. I see them staring out the window watching the kids play. Then I feel their angry eyes on me. "Stupid," I hear one kid in the front whisper.

This scene happens every day. Would it bother you?

Catharine Grace is a graduate of the Threshold Program at Lesley College. The story is her reflection on her early school experiences written for an assignment at Lesley.

Chapter 2

Young Adult Voices

A s children with learning disabilities grow older, memories of school experiences are often softened by the passage of time. The overall pain is lessened. High points and low points tend to stand out: the kind teacher who understood, the struggle to get through high school sociology, the understanding friends and the not-so-understanding ones.

Remarkably, many of these high school graduates would not change their lives even if they could. They state that the uphill battles have made them stronger and have shaped their characters and personalities in unique and now comfortable ways.

College and young adulthood is an important time for these individuals to begin to figure out who they are and to understand their place in the world. The "disability" labels, once useful in helping to validate their frustrations and struggles, now become confining and no longer seem to fit their view of themselves. They have succeeded in getting through school, and therefore they do not feel "disabled." They have proved to themselves and to others that they were and are "able," and they are proud of it. They can look back and reflect on the past but can also look ahead to a future they will shape on their own.

As one contributor, Avi Ostchega, noted, "I hope to exemplify the notion that there truly is a light at the end of the twisted road on which these kids travel . . . . These children and young adults will discover passage past frustration and pain that will lead to a higher understanding of their own minds and abilities."

They are willing to acknowledge the role their parents and teachers played in getting them this far. However, they know that from now on they will have to serve as their own advocates.

The voices in this chapter speak to the emergence of self-acceptance and pride and an even greater determination to succeed.

Days

by Avi Ostchega

Days, we have good days and bad days,

Some days you feel alive and well,

   radiating positive energy

Some days the world closes in around you

Some days you seek the knowledge that can only be

   gained in careful study

Some days feel more like nights

Some days just don't feel

Some days are fun

Some days you can take on the world

Some days you miss loved ones more with each minute

Some days you feel close to your friends

Some days are friendless and void

Some days are young

Some days are old

One day has a ground hog

Some days are dry

Some days are wet

Some days are gray

Some days you must

Some days you mustn't

Some days you lust

Some days you stay warm in bed

Some days you run from the police

Some days may be your last days

So don't count days, but live them

Avi Ostchega wrote this poem during his first year at Montgomery College. He plans to attend law school after college. This poem was printed in the January 1994 Parents of Gifted/LD Children Newsletter. *Another work by Avi can be found in chapter 4. He lives in Maryland.*

Follow the Road

by Jessica Lenz

Follow the road to a brighter horizon,

Where dreams come alive by a twitch of your eye.

The journey is challenging, falling is expected,

But you can succeed if you're willing to try.

Love and affection you'll find on this journey,

Expect flying colors to flash by your eyes.

Congratulations, you've finally made it,

To your brighter horizon and a happier today.

Jessica Lenz is a graduate of the Threshold Program at Lesley College. Throughout school she had difficulties in the auditory and visual areas. She is now a nursing assistant in Massachusetts.

Being Without and Losing Out

by Andrea Rose Schneider

Take heed, I need the speed with which to read as everyone does; my hindrances are many, that I lack in endurance
and accuracy—I take my hand at what skills I can acquire in
the land I live, but by what recourse praytell can you advise,
the size is but little there, for I compare these skills that are
made for you are not nil, for you who have the normal cell
structures, this punctures, giving way to a hole in my development, which no government hath the strength or will to mend
and tend to for they are without knowledge—to heal those
they do not understand and would rather brand.

*Andrea Rose Schneider has a mild hearing loss and learning disabilities in
reading, math, and organization. She is in a master's program in Special
Education at Boston University and utilizes the learning disabilities support
services. This poem was originally published by the National Library of Poetry, Maryland, in the book* Windows on the World, *vol. 2, 1992. Andrea
advises, "Life is a struggle, but not to extremes. If you need, pause and then
go on." She is from New York.*

Proudest Moments

by Kay Lipper

One of my proudest moments was during home room in high school. I was called to the office over the loud speaker. On my way down to the office, I kept thinking what did I do? Am I in trouble?

I got to the office door thinking okay get it over with. It can't be that bad. I walked through the door, and my mother was leaning against the counter, and she said, "Hi, college student." When I heard this, I jumped up on my mom in shock. I could not believe it.

So I went and told the teachers that helped me get into Threshold. After I told them, they looked at me in shock, and said, "You're kidding!"

I think my mother was more excited than me. After she told me, she drove downtown and told everybody she could find that I got into college. This is not to say that she did not believe I couldn't get into college, but she was so proud of me. That is why she did that.

My other proudest moment was when I graduated from high school. I had mixed feelings about it. On the one hand, I was upset about leaving the teachers who were my best friends. On the other hand, I was happy and excited because I got into college. For the first time in a long while, something was going right in our family life. What I mean by this is that my family forgot about all their pain, and we had some happiness in our lives, which I personally did not mind at all.

On graduation day I was so scared because I was ending a part of my life that had not been good, but it had not been that bad. I would be starting a whole new scary life in college with total strangers. You know, it is kind of funny, that my proudest moments were my most scary moments.

Kay Lipper is a graduate of the Threshold Program at Lesley College. She had memory and math difficulties throughout school but remained in mainstream classes. She now works in Massachusetts as a home health aide to the elderly.

My Book Says God

by Kristina Kops

The events surrounding one of the most influential cir-
cumstances in my life began in the first grade when I was
learning how to read. Sitting at the front of my classroom, I
began to read out loud slowly and steadily, "The boy looked
down at his God."

"Dog," corrected my teacher.

"No, my book says God," I said in my defense.

"No, it says dog," insisted my teacher.

Finally, when I looked at the word for the fourth time, I
realized it said dog. This was the first of many reversals that
eventually, with the development of better learning analysis,
led to the diagnosis of a visual spatial learning disability in the
seventh grade.

At that time there seemed to be two ways for my family to
look at my disability, either as a limitation that was always
going to hold me back, or as a challenging obstacle that could
be overcome. Since I had accomplished at such a high level
before I ever knew I had a learning disability, the latter choice
seemed the appropriate outlook for us to have. Because of the
positive support of my parents who were always there to help
when I needed it, I saw this as a problem that I had to deal
with and then continue. My attitude was captured by Nike in
their advertisements, "Just do it."

The months that followed were a rebuilding period during
which I tried to understand my difficulty and re-organize my
learning style. Receiving additional time on tests allowed me
the chance to prove what I actually knew. I learned how to
keep my place on multiple choice tests as well as how to catch
my mistakes. New study techniques such as flash cards helped
me to make my studying time more efficient and effective. My

ability to reaccustom myself to a new speed of working and becoming comfortable with the fact that my work was going to take longer than it did other people, were keys to my success. Most of all, I needed to learn not to be embarrassed by my differences, and to just keep doing what I needed to, whether or not others understood. Often, others didn't believe that someone with such good grades could really have a learning disability. They didn't know the work I put in to get those grades. I finally realized that only I needed to know. Gradually, I learned how to keep my mistakes at a minimum, to compensate for my disability and to ask for minimal assistance when absolutely necessary.

I learned many things from this experience. I learned to be a self advocate and self evaluator. These skills allow me not to be afraid to make changes if they are needed, and to appreciate when things are working well. The personal awareness I have gained has given me the self confidence I need to succeed. I now see my disability as an enhancing factor rather than a limiting one. The extra time I need to complete my work is no longer extra time but necessary time. These adaptation skills and self confidence are now a permanent part of me that I can take with me to college and beyond. My learning disability has never been used as an excuse, but rather as a catalyst for more creative and successful ways to learn.

Kristina Kops wrote this essay as part of her college application process. She lives in Connecticut.

Untitled

by Catharine Grace

Ever since I was six years old I always knew in my heart and mind that I wished for nothing more than to be an artist.

When I was younger, I was terrible at math and science. I had nightmares about going to my fifth grade math class, while we were learning about fractions. I was upset because unlike everyone else I still couldn't get it.

At the same time that I was fearful about math I was winning state wide art competitions. I was nominated best artist of my junior high school and my classmates were impressed with my doodling skills and drawings (especially they enjoyed the drawings of my math teacher). Yes, I felt terrible about my lack of knowledge in subjects that seemed to me to be more important than art. Well sure math and science had to be more important than art, right? I always did think that, but now I think differently.

After all these years of feeling ashamed and disappointed, I feel my life has turned out pretty good. After being picked on as a little kid because of my differences, I am a much stronger adult. I feel I am much more independent, stronger emotionally than many of my peers who didn't have learning disabilities. Many of my friends who were good at math and science and got good grades are still living at home, and finding life rather tough for the first time. I've been living on my own for four years now and I'm just twenty-five years old.

My friends understand why I brought that up, because they all say they wish they could be more independent like me.

I'm writing all of this to express to parents that whatever their child's situation may be, it's not hopeless at all. Things will definitely work themselves out, just don't get too stressed out in the meantime. Your child will pick up on that, and it may make them feel bad about themselves, even though there is no intention on either parent's part for that to happen.

For teachers my advice is to be more sensitive towards students with LD, but not to make them feel totally different from other students.

For kids with LD things aren't as bad as they seem, your life will definitely get better as the years go on. Try not to focus all of your attention on it. Try and find something that you're really good at, and enjoy doing that. While at the same time not ignoring the things that are an issue in your life. Just don't get caught up in it and remember that things will come together, and you will wonder why you got so upset about not being able to do a fraction. Find what you are good at and pursue it.

I think that people with learning disabilities are very strong individuals and that others can learn a lot from us.

Catharine Grace, a graduate of the Threshold Program at Lesley College, is hoping to pursue a career as an artist. She lives in Massachusetts. An earlier work by Catharine appears in chapter 1.

Untitled

by Elizabeth Upsher

From the beginning of my education, I was always having trouble. Mrs. M, my kindergarten teacher, wrote to my mother, telling her that I never paid attention in school. My second and third grade teachers complained that I talked back, and never tried to learn; that I never seemed interested in anything. When the class learned how to tell time, I didn't learn with them. I didn't understand how, and the more questions I asked, the more frustrated the teacher and I became. Finally, I taught myself how to read a clock and how to tell time without help from anyone. I remember sitting with a teacher's aide, I remember trying to learn the difference between my b's and d's, I remember many days before and after school at math extra help, and I remember too many C's and D's. My mother sent me to a private school in the seventh grade, where the work was abundant and difficult. By this time in my education, I no longer expected teachers to be able to help me with things I didn't understand, and because of my frustration, I often did not try in school, becoming content with a C average. Reports still came from my teachers calling me lazy and inconsistent.

After my ninth grade year, a psychologist suggested that I have testing done; maybe my bad grades in school weren't my fault. My IQ, my standardized test scores and my obvious intelligence when writing and speaking suggested that I was a lot smarter than my grades indicated. Extensive testing confirmed that I was learning disabled. Further examination in my Junior year of high school showed that I also had ADD (Attention Deficit Disorder). These things explained my short attention span, my frustration in school since kindergarten and my inability to learn basic skills such as telling time.

It was only several years ago that people began to study learning disabilities. Even today, when there are special classes and more equality for kids with learning disabilities, some people don't believe such a thing exists. Instead, many people believe that Attention Deficit is an excuse for kids who haven't done well in school, or who get in trouble a lot because they don't care. Some people use it as an excuse, but not me, because I'm angry. I'm angry at the teachers who called me lazy and who never wondered why I might be that way. I'm angry that I struggled through almost ten years of school and that nobody ever noticed that I was a smart kid. I do know, however, that dwelling on the lack of understanding of the teachers in my past won't help.

The best thing I can do now is to stand up for myself and be responsible in making sure I understand everything in my classes and make sure I don't get left behind. I have learned how to study at home, how to learn in class, and how to keep asking questions when I don't understand something. Sometimes I wonder: what would have happened if I had never learned to tell time?

Elizabeth Upsher wrote this essay as part of her college application. She lives in Connecticut.

So What!

by Lynne McCarthy

So we're not as smart as someone else. Who cares? We manage to live and work in the real world. That's all that's important. Do you have to know algebra, Romeo and Juliet, biology? I say all you need to know is the basics in life— money, tell time, tie your shoe.

People who like to make fun of other people such as us are only bragging. It's like a pretty girl in high school who is very popular with the guys. She might make fun of a girl who has no boyfriends and is not so pretty. She's saying, "Ha, Ha, I'm prettier and more popular." These people are saying, "Ha, Ha, I'm smarter."

Maybe they wish they weren't so smart. "I'd get more attention if I weren't so smart. People would feel sorry for me." It's not true, but maybe that's what they think. Maybe not? Who knows. Different people think differently. But, all I can say is when they tease, they are putting themselves down . . . .

The world would be very boring if everyone was the same. I'm glad I'm different. I can survive in this world; I'm living; I'm different; I have a whole different personality than anyone else. So don't be depressed. Forget about any problems you might have and just smile. You got a reason to be happy. You're alive and you're surviving. So, Smile!

Lynne McCarthy wrote this at age 18 while she was a student in the Threshold Program at Lesley College. She wrote it to express her disagreement with others who believe in hiding handicaps. She lives in Massachusetts.

Where Does the Time Go?

by Jesse W. Adcox

Where does the time go?

>That's what I'd like to know.

>Not about dinosaurs or foreign wars, dirty tasks or

unwanted

>>chores.

Where does the time go?

>That's something I'd like to ask.

>Not about ancient fights or King Arthur's Knights or

>>prehistoric civil rights.

Where does the time go?

>Because that's a place I'd like to be.

>And stroll down the lane and look through the pain to a

>>forgotten memory.

Jesse Adcox, a student at Hofstra University, attended Landmark College in Vermont. He wrote this poem because he felt his life was flying by too quickly and had no direction. Jesse lives in Connecticut and dedicates this poem to Linda DeMotta.

Speaking Up

by Kimberly Harter-Key

The proudest moment of my life was in high school when I yelled at my sociology teacher. Just those few short moments made me realize what kind of person I am. It was a little after the beginning of the year, and on that day I had sought out my teacher, Mr. M., to explain a homework assignment to me more clearly. Instead of showing interest for my problem, he ended up criticizing me for my disabilities and telling me I was too illiterate to be in his class. I really couldn't believe what he was saying. I ran out of the school office in tears.

I went to find my speech teacher, Mrs. W., who had always been there for me when I had a problem. I finally found her in a separate part of the school. Through my tears, I told Mrs. W. what Mr. M. had said. She was also amazed at how he had reacted in the situation. She even arranged a time when we all could meet.

All three of us met in her room that Friday to discuss the problem. I actually yelled at him and told him how he discriminated against me because I was a little different from the rest of the class. I had decided that I would *never* let him see me cry, but I was so upset at that moment that I didn't care. At that moment, I was upset to the point where I didn't care about anything else. As I was going through all the words, I was surprised at myself for having the courage to say all of this to my teacher.

After he left, I saw that Mrs. W. was crying. I asked her what was wrong. She just hugged me and said she couldn't have handled it better than I did.

Up until this day, I have never understood why I reacted in such a way that I overcame someone in authority over me. I must expect myself to surprise myself at certain times.

Kimberly Harter-Key wrote this while she was in the Threshold Program at Lesley College. She now lives in Massachusetts with her husband and two children.

ADD: What's It Like?

by Robert Wilson

When you're ADD, your thoughts go bouncing around in your head like a ping-pong ball. Trying to harness your thoughts and keep them on one thing is very difficult. It is very frustrating because you really want to keep your mind on something and, no matter how hard you try, you can't. Anything you do takes a long time because your mind wanders and things take longer than they should. It has taken me about 4 minutes to write this much, and my mind has wandered about 6 or 7 times since I started writing. One problem is that when you hear something, it makes you think of 10 other things related, if only vaguely, to it. For example, when I wrote the words "Since I started writing" (above) the word "writing" somehow made me think of the "Wright Brothers," which made me think of my vacation to England a few years ago (since I took an airplane there) which made me think of Henry the 8th, which made me think I'd like a piece of cake right now, which reminded me of an exhibit at the San Diego Zoo where they had a large cake with some kind of mice that had actually made little homes in it (no kidding) and that reminded me that I saw a mouse in the backyard yesterday, and that made me wonder how my gladioluses (glads) are doing, which made me think of a commercial for Glad plastic bags . . . . You get the idea? The problem is that this is uncontrollable. This goes on all the time when I am in class listening, or trying to listen, to lectures. What's worse is that this can happen any time, so you may miss something useless or you may miss something important. A person with ADD is often very forgetful. Not that they have bad memories, but they forget things in the short term. An instructor of mine once marveled that I could remember detailed facts about one thing or another and relate them in class, but I could forget what she had said a few seconds before. I, for example, can be searching for my car keys while they are in my hand. I've walked out of restaurants without paying (just forgot . . .) and when I'm writing papers or things like this I'll often forget what the point of my sentence was before I get done writing it.

Robert Wilson was 23 years old and in his senior year of college when he wrote the above. He has attention deficit disorder. He lives in California.

Key to Life

by Julie Daniels

You have a key to life.

If you take the key to life, you can open the doors to life and

have many opportunities.

If you lock your doors to life, then you can't open your doors

to learn.

Then you won't go anywhere.

Julie Daniels is a graduate of the Threshold Program, Lesley College and wrote this as part of her course work. She lives in Massachusetts.

Some Teachers Really Did Make a Difference

by Chris Reilly

I can remember standing in front of the class at the blackboard in third grade. I was having a tough time with figuring out a math problem that I was doing. The whole class was watching me and I could hear kids saying that I was so stupid because I could not figure out the problem. The part of school that I hated the most was on Friday when everyone had to get up in front of the class and do a math problem. As I stood there trying to figure it out it was getting frustrating for me. I tried my hardest to get it right but as usual got it wrong. When I walked back to my seat kids made comments to me as I walked by them. They said things like, "When God was giving out brains you thought he said *trains* and you took the first one out of town." It really ate me up inside that I could not do well in school like my classmates. I wanted so much to fit in but really didn't. I don't think the teacher was trying to make a fool out of me but she was doing a good job of it. I will never forget always trying my hardest to do well but never being able to succeed. . . .

One thing that saved me (later on) was athletics. If I didn't have that I would have given up somewhere along the way. But being good at something really made a difference in my life and hockey was my answer. I always played a couple of levels above my age group because I was so good. This made me mature faster than most of my friends because I always had to act older to fit in with the older kids. . . . I tell you it was quite scary when you are playing against someone who is a senior and a full grown man and you're just a kid who is 14 years old trying to survive. I would have to say that it was a great self-esteem builder. . . .

There were some teachers that really did make a difference in my life all throughout this period (middle and high school) of my academic career. My history teacher Dr. R. really made a difference for me with learning. He was one of the first teachers that I had that truly cared about his students. I did really well in his class and he always had praise for my work. He knew it was tough for me to succeed but he set it up so I would. Another teacher was Mr. J.R. He not only taught me about science but about money and the stock market. Even after he was done teaching me he was teaching me because I went to work for him at his company. The last of my great teachers from that day was Mr. C. He taught me English all through high school. He really took the time to go over my work and show me what I did wrong and how not to make the same mistake again. He was also the first teacher that I had who said I was smart and would succeed in life. I owe a great deal to these men for helping me get through school.

The one person who did make the most impact on me and taught me not to quit, no matter how hard things got was Mr. D. He was my tutor from seventh grade until the last day of high school. He was the best thing that could have happened to me outside of my teachers. I feel without him I would never have graduated from high school. He believed in me and showed me ways to compensate for my disability so I could succeed in school. He took the time to explain things to me and made everything clear.

Chris Reilly wrote this after graduating from college. It was originally printed in the 1992 edition of Their World *and is reprinted with permission.*

Life with Learning Disabilities

by Ellen Federman

When someone asked me to describe myself with a learning disability, I described myself as dumb and stupid. When asked why I described myself as dumb and stupid, I replied, "I guess because I feel that way." All my life I've felt that way.

It was nine o'clock on a Sunday. I lay on my bed thinking about Monday and how I didn't want to get up for school. Monday came and faking a sickness was better than withstanding the torture I felt when I went to school. The work was one thing but when lunch and recess came, I found myself eating alone and playing outside alone. I never had anyone to play with. At times it got so bad that I liked playing with kids younger than me because I felt they accepted me.

Ever since I was little, I had dreams and fantasies about how my life should go and, most of all, how I wished my life would go. I was always smart, beautiful and had a lot of friends. In my fantasies, everything came easily to me no matter what it was, especially socially and academically.

It's May 3, 1971. Ellen Anne Federman was born 5 pounds and 6 ounces. Was she healthy? Was she normal? At such an early age, it was hard to tell. Each child develops at different speeds, even when normal. When I was a very young age, I had trouble sitting. Every time I'd look up to see a person, my eyes were closed up so much that I had to look all the way up and toppled over a lot. Soon after lots of toppling over, I finally mastered it. What was wrong with me? Why was I like this? . . . .

As I grew older and older, my life got harder and harder. The work in school became increasingly more difficult. I found that the way I looked and how I did in school affected me socially. I was always made fun of, so much so that I became passive and more depressed than ever. My parents knew how upset I was, but there is just so much parents can do. I mean you love your children and get heartbroken whenever anyone hurts your child. It's hard to deal with.

Academically my grades were awful. D's and F's were about all I could pull off. My parents were frustrated and so were my teachers. No matter how hard I tried, I couldn't excel in anything that had to do with school.

People couldn't believe I had a learning disability because when I sat down at the piano, I could play beautifully. Or when they'd look at me, people would say, "Gee, you don't look like you have a learning disability!" You know I never thought that having a learning problem made a person look a certain way. I always thought it had something to do with a messed up brain. I also never thought someone could look at and automatically say, "Well, she definitely has a learning disability." Another person would reply, "How do you know?" "She looks like she has one." "How does she look?" "I don't exactly know." It's been that way all my life academically and socially.

When I was at school, whenever the teacher went any-where near the door, I'd panic. I could just see the other kids on the edge of their seats, just waiting for the teacher to leave so they could have a roasting. The teacher would leave and they would make fun of me. Each would take their turn with me—fun huh? I, being my passive self, let people do it to me. When I got home I would do a role play of what guts I had then to tell them off, but when the next day came, the same thing happened. I never said a word.

Teachers continually said the same things about me to my parents. "She's being lazy!" How could I be being lazy when whenever I sat down for hours on end trying as hard as I could to learn something, it would draw a blank in my brain. The only thing that made me tired was the emotional aspect of it.

When I was young I was sent to a hospital. The hospital

was a hospital for the research of learning disabilities and kids with coordination problems. All the tests I took and all the days off from school never showed anything but that I had a learning disability. All those days I pleaded with my parents to let me stay home and not go through the same testing each time with no breaks. I always felt dumb and stupid and felt different. I felt embarrassed. The thing about the testing was it never went anywhere. My learning disability wasn't helped by the testing. . . .

Two people in my life I love very much are my parents. I always wondered how they felt and dealt with my disability. I know it must have been hard for them. When they would put me though testing or when they would send me to school knowing how much I hated it, I could see the pain in their eyes. I knew there was only so much they could do. They were so strong. They were there for me when I needed them most. Sometimes I wondered if they ever got frustrated with me. Did they ever think they did something wrong? Did they cry at night? But each time I feel they were there to help me up. Mom, Dad, I love you. Parents of learning disabled children have the hardest job. They have to help the children to be strong and to be strong themselves. I admire their strength. . . .

When I applied to college, I only applied to one college which was Lesley College's Threshold Program in Cambridge, Massachusetts. It seemed to be the best school for me. I applied and hoped and prayed for an acceptance. I went for an interview and I felt pretty confident about the interview. I was nervous about getting in. I think my parents were even more nervous. After long months of waiting, they called and HAD accepted me.

I now attend my first year at college, which many people thought was impossible for me. At times it gets hard with all the responsibilities, but people with learning disabilities can do it. Any goal we set within reason we can accomplish if we try hard enough. My parents taught me that. Out of all the things my parents taught me, that always stuck in my mind as something I'll always remember and follow for the rest of my life. I am going to work hard and achieve the goals I desire and deserve. Being learning disabled doesn't mean that life is over. For those teachers who told me that I couldn't do certain things, just wait and when I am successful, you will see.

Ellen Federman authored this at age 21 while she was enrolled in the Threshold Program, Lesley College. She has overcome her insecurities and is working toward a bachelor's degree in Special Education. She does not consider herself disabled. Ellen lives in Massachusetts.

No One Can Tell

by Heather Susan Schwam

Behind her smile, no one can tell.

Behind her eyes lies a sea of despair.

An ocean in which she drowned in.

She thought she could fly.

She thought she could swim.

She thought she could try.

She thought she could win.

Beyond the laughter, she hides her tears.

Deep down she cries and hides her fears.

No one can tell it's between me and you.

No one can tell, can you?

During a postgraduate program at Riverview School, nineteen-year-old Heather Schwam was asked to describe her feelings in relation to her learning disabilities. She wrote the above poem in response. She says, "Being LD is not a crime, it's an experience." Heather lives in Connecticut.

High School Graduation

by Margaret Birch

I put on my cap and gown and started to cry. Part of my battle was over. My father came in and gave me a kiss. Then, thinking back, I remembered something my grandfather told me before he died. He said, "My little Margie, you'll reach for the stars and you'll get them."

I got in the car and went to school. I saw my friends. We all went into a huge hug. Then it was time to march. I walked with the other graduates remembering words I heard before from my school principal. "You'll never graduate from high school." I proved her wrong.

Then awards were over. We marched to get our diplomas. I got mine and found out I graduated with honors. I started to walk out with the graduates and my house master hugged me and said, "You fought a hard battle." Then I saw my mother crying and I knew at that moment I could handle life on my own.

Margaret Birch composed this while she was a student in the Threshold Program at Lesley College. She is working on her associate's degree at Fisher College and is no longer ashamed about having a learning disability. She lives in Massachusetts.

Untitled

by Darren Hines

When I entered the second grade my parents found out that I had a learning disability. When I was younger, being LD didn't bother me. However, when I entered elementary school my concern became not being with my friends because I needed special attention in my education. Maybe the difference between then and now was understanding. Then I didn't understand what being LD meant. I went through denial, depression, and frustration. . . .

A state of denial would exist until the late years of high school. Nevertheless, I never stopped trying to overcome this disability. . . . While I protected myself from letting people know of my problems I would also be causing myself frustration, not only in hiding my problem but causing myself to receive poor grades that I could have prevented.

Times have changed and I now realize that I can't change the fact that I am LD, but I can take advantage of programs that help. The frustration will still exist. The fact is it's harder for me to understand what the "normal" person can understand without much thought, and every so often the depression touches down when I try and try to understand something or when people (mainly teachers who don't understand LD) won't go over something a couple more times so I can understand or try to teach me a different way. But now I'm confident that I can learn most things if I keep trying and have teachers who know how to teach me, taking advantage of my strengths.

This excerpt is taken from an essay Darren Hines wrote during his senior year of high school for his college application. He was a student at the Oakland School. Darren lives in Virginia.

Discovering Paths

by Kate Shannon

The paths I seek are taken,

and I have to choose my own way.

I get angered and confused about that.

On the road of experience,

I have discovered I can seek my own path.

I have chosen the untraveled road,

the road unused.

In the universe, it is difficult to find new paths.

It is like seeking out something very dark and distant.

Yet you can see the light if you look,

but only in the distance.

When you have had experience taking the wrong turns,

you tend to learn to think ahead of time,

so you won't get lost again.

Kate Shannon, a graduate of the Threshold Program at Lesley College, wrote this while she was in the program. She lives in Maryland.

Chapter 3

Adult Voices

T his chapter should provide the definitive answer to the question asked most often by parents: "Will my child grow out of it?" Well-meaning professionals and nonprofessionals, in their attempt to provide comfort and consolation, might mislead parents by answering "Yes." As the writings on the following pages show, individuals do not outgrow their disabilities; rather, they learn to grow *with* them and to accommodate them. Some even capitalize on a learning disability and use it to their advantage. They have come to terms with their learning disability and refuse to let it control their lives.

Technology has developed to the benefit of people who learn and function differently. In today's world, how often do people balance a checkbook without using a calculator, write a letter without using a typewriter or computer, or even check their own spelling without using a spell-checker?

Adults with learning disabilities have learned which tools they need in order to be efficient. They write notes and lists to help them remember what to do. They buy phones with memory so that they can store numbers they are likely to forget. They surround themselves with friends who are understanding and accepting. They choose occupations that maximize their strengths and minimize their weaknesses. They learn to laugh at their mistakes and take pride in their triumphs. Their problems have not changed, but their way of viewing them has.

Many of them call on their own experiences to help others through theirs. The adults whose stories are on the following pages understand the difficult times and frustrations that children and adolescents are having, because they've been there themselves. They have not grown *out* of their disabilities, they have grown *up*. And in many cases, they contend that they are better people for having gone through the difficult times and survived. As one contributor, Nancy Edwards Clay, explains, "In retrospect, I can see that those qualities that made me feel so different and defective back then are the very qualities that make my life so rich and interesting now. . . . It may be a rough ride sometimes, but I wouldn't trade places with anyone."

Their voices are loud and clear. These people have learned to like and accept themselves as they are, and they serve as an inspiration to those who come after them.

Living with a Learning Disability

by Kathleen Holmes

I first heard about dyslexia while watching a television commentary. The symptoms described were exactly the difficulties I have experienced. For example, I confuse letters such as m with w, n with u, b with d, or p with q, and digits in numbers such as 245 for 254 or 1856 for 1865. This confusion applied to dates in history as well as numbers in math and science. It also led to transposition of notes when reading music and word problems using numbers and letters such as those in scientific equations and directions, whether written or spoken, in any subject. Today, I have found an explanation and a willingness to share my frustration. I have a language communication disability, dyslexia.

I am a 39-year-old African American female, married with one son 21 years of age. Most of my working adulthood I have worked in offices and provided academic and various social services in positions ranging from secretary to program director. My job functions always included reading, writing and much speaking. Since 1959, I have attended grade school (grades K through 12), business and clerical school (1 year 6 months), computer training school (1 year), 4 colleges over a span of 15 years and various seminars, conferences and workshops in supervisory and management training. I have also attended special interest classes and training for hobbies in art and music. But through it all I have had one deep secret so hidden that I just accepted that I wasn't good enough, smart enough, fast enough to compete academically. . . .

While in elementary school, I was usually placed in basic reading classes to improve my reading speed and comprehension. . . . Since I was not able to finish the exams within the time allotted, the unanswered questions would be counted as incorrect and I was graded below the standard for that grade. . . . I always made average to above average grades in all subjects except reading. My dyslexia had been misdiagnosed, and my intellect underestimated. I learned not to be discouraged by low grades but to continue to pursue my education.

After viewing the television commentary on dyslexia, I telephoned the National Association on Dyslexia in Baltimore, Maryland, and was seen by a psychologist on staff. . . . I was given various tests. . . .

I was also asked questions about my self-esteem. At this point I cried as I explained how painful it has been to live with this disorder and be told I was lazy or didn't concentrate on what I was doing. I hid this disorder by asking others to assist me with my written work or just avoided writing, reading books and articles to prevent the sleepiness and headaches that are also common to dyslexics and to avoid condescending remarks from people.

After writing this essay and reassessing my learning experiences, I now feel more receptive to my personality type, "INTP—The Journalist" (according to the Kerisey Sorter). I have adapted to building on my strengths and favorable personality traits such as patience and compassion. I also have a love for learning and eagerness to spend a lifetime discovering more and sharing my knowledge with others. . . .

I literally laughed and denied that I could possibly become a journalist. I can see where it takes great creative and illustrative ability that I possess but I lacked confidence because of the dyslexia. I can also see how my developing a positive attitude towards challenges in life has allowed me to have a greater concern for helping others to discover their strengths and to live life more fully. I plan to pursue my creative writing skills further and to continue to attain my goals in the future.

The above is an excerpt from an essay Kathleen Holmes wrote both as a petition for academic credit for experiential learning and as a class assignment. She received a grade of A+ on the essay, which has since become part of her personal portfolio. She is a full-time student and lives in Georgia.

The List

by Mary Daum

As I looked in the mirror this morning,
my reflection sternly advised,
"You're going to make some changes today,
and get yourself organized."
"Now that's a novel idea,"
I thought as I combed my hair.
So I'll search the house for the notebook
that I placed—somewhere.
As soon as I find that notebook,
I'll make the greatest list
Of all the things I need to do,
but somehow always missed.

I'll take each item one by one
and finish each thing I've started.
I'll concentrate and focus,
and chaos will be outsmarted.
I'll tell myself to concentrate
and search for that notebook.
Methodically I'll give each room
an extra careful look.

The living room needs dusting,
that will only take a minute.
So I went to the linen closet,
and found there's nothing in it.
Looks like I need to do laundry,
I think with a sense of gloom.
So I grab a laundry basket
and head for the laundry room.

As I walk down the hallway,
laundry basket in one hand,
I notice the kids have dropped their shoes
wherever they might land.
I pick up the shoes and take them
to the place where they belong.
As I open the door to the bedroom
I'm feeling calm and strong.

I see the mess in the kids' room
and now I'm feeling blue.
I'll take a minute and straighten up,
that's just what I'll do.
I find my daughter's artwork
sitting on the bedroom floor,
and take it to the kitchen
to display it on the fridge's door.

The fridge reminds me I'm hungry
so I fix a little snack.
I notice I need to buy groceries,
so I'm off to the store and back.
I bought a new magazine,
so I sit down and take a break.
I realize I've dozed off
when the phone startles me awake.

And on and on it goes
as my organized day progresses.
I jump from room to room,
getting started on various messes.
And suddenly it's dinnertime
and the day has just flown by.
I never found that notebook
or made my list, I wonder why . . .

The living room's still dusty,
and the laundry isn't done.
I've started a hundred projects,
but haven't completed one.
I think about this crazy day
and suddenly realized
That I really must do something
to get myself organized.

As I brush my teeth at bedtime,
my reflection stares sternly at me.
"Relax," I say to the girl in the mirror.
"Tomorrow I'll be orderly."

Mary Daum has attention deficit disorder (ADD) and publishes a newsletter for those living with ADD called ADD-ONS. She lives in Illinois.

If I'm Smart, Why do I FEEL so STUPID?

by Liz Welker

I stared at my algebra book and finally slammed it shut. What was wrong with me? I had studied for hours—DAYS—for that test, and failed. In fact, I had failed brutally. It made no sense to me at all. I had never had trouble with math before; in fact, math was always one of my better subjects until algebra. I had struggled through it in high school, and I always felt that I was smart and learned quickly until I studied for days at a time and began to fail. Did I have a shunt blockage? I didn't think so, because I felt fine. I had dealt with hydrocephalus, or "water on the brain," as it was commonly called, all my life, and I knew what it felt like when the shunt, the silicone-rubber tube that drained the fluid inside my head into the stomach cavity, was shutting down. I felt no discomfort. So WHY was I having so much trouble learning? Why did I have to struggle so hard in high school algebra and biology?

I had to struggle like that, I later learned, because I had three learning disabilities. They were spatial, perception, and logic. I was 20 years old before I found out, and at the time, it was believed that I had as many as a DOZEN LD's. I knew I couldn't possibly have had so many, because some of the problems I was having, which were later proven to be due to a severe reaction to epilepsy medication, were new to me in college. When I was finally taken off the medication and put on something that I tolerated much better, the problems with math directions, and other things like my memory and concentration were, unfortunately, still there. I was able, however, to recover some of the memory and studied better as a result. Once again, I began to excel in English and other classes with which I had never before had trouble. These, I found out, were, in fact, LD's. They were not going to "go away" by taking another medication, or even by my being withdrawn from medication, as I found out after being off everything for six months. I couldn't "think" them away. I couldn't "concentrate" them away. I simply had to deal with them.

The hardest part of learning about and dealing with LD's, I think, was educating myself and others, like my father, on what they were. When I told Dad, he cried, "You're not stupid!" He was right. I wasn't. I was simply unable to learn in the same way and timeframe that most other students could. In fact, for that reason, I prefer to call them "learning DIFFICULTIES," because I CAN learn; it just takes a lot of work and more time. Eventually, in spite of the medication problem, which lasted nearly three years, I was able to get a "C" in College Algebra and complete my degree.

I found that, just as I had learned to feel better the more I learned about my condition, the more easily I was able to compensate for my learning problems and help my family understand them as well. My father has expressed sincere regret for his comment, although I am aware that he was never taught otherwise until I explained to him what having LD's meant. I still dread going to places I've never been before and having to drive home, because I get lost so easily, and I hope I never see another algebra book again, but I proved to myself, my teachers, and my family that success with LD's IS possible.

Liz Welker is a 27-year-old mother whose LD's are slow thought process, slow comprehension, spatial difficulty, poor short-term memory, and absence of logical thinking. Professionals told her, "You never should have expected to go to college." She took college algebra four times and finally passed and got her degree. Liz lives in Virginia.

Driving Ambition

by Jim H. Shreve

My first driving lesson was on the family tractor. After a heavy rain, our dirt road would become a rutted mess. After it had dried sufficiently, Dad would get the tractor out to *drag the road*. That is, pull a contraption behind the tractor to level the road and smooth out the ruts. After dragging the road this time, he put the drag away and told me to jump onto the seat. Great! I was going to drive the tractor! Well, it turned out to be pretty simple. You just put it into the proper gear, let up on the clutch and off I went. It was almost impossible to stall. I drove around our property for a while thinking, "I'm doing it. I'm driving the tractor, Oboyoboyboy."

Everything was going great until I heard those words ring out "Now, let's see you back up." Gulp. "How do I do this?" I stopped the tractor and looked down at the shifter. OK, push in the clutch, shift into reverse, let up the clutch. Suddenly, I thought, "How do I watch where I am going?" I have to watch my feet when I am working the clutch, otherwise I won't know what they are doing. Then I have to sit facing straight forward so that my hands can work the steering wheel. How do I see what's behind me? I tried just turning my head enough to look over my shoulder with one eye. That didn't work. I could not see directly behind me. Dad kept telling me to look behind me, couldn't he see that I was trying? I could turn around and look if I didn't have to steer. Suddenly the lesson was over. Once again, I did something wrong. I didn't know what, but something. That was the last time that I was allowed to drive the tractor. *Why do these things always happen to me?*

I remember well my first attempt at learning to drive a car. My dad took me out in a car with a stick shift. Dad would feed me instructions one at a time. Thank goodness the car was pointed toward the road. I did not have to back it out of the parking space. It had been years since the tractor experience, but I had not forgotten what driving backwards was like. I got the car started, eased it into gear, and let up on the clutch, *clunk*. I could see right off the bat that this clutch thing was not going to be easy. Finally I got the car out of the parking space and down the road. All too quickly, Dad told me that it was time to shift again.

I knew what to do. Put one foot on the clutch, move the gear shift to the other gear, and move the foot off the clutch while pressing harder on the gas pedal with the other foot. That didn't sound too complicated. OK, down on the left foot, move the stick, "ease up slowly," my dad said suddenly, his words crashing through my head like a runaway semi-truck. "Look at the road, ease up on the clutch, give it more gas." The barrage of words continued to rain down upon me. Surely, I didn't want this to end in a crash. *Clunk*. The car died right there in the street. The words continued, "You have to ease up on the clutch, give it more gas, watch the road. . . ." My head was spinning, "Why can't the words just stop?"

I thought to myself, "I know what I have to do, why can't I just go to an empty lot by myself and practice it. Without cars around me, without trying to stay on the road, without someone talking to me." But that was not to be. OK, let me try this. Move the left leg up slowly, hold on to the steering wheel, move the right leg down slowly, *clunk*. I never did get that car into third gear. The lesson was cut short. I managed to get the car back home. At least the ride home was quiet. That was the end of driving lessons in that car.

Jim H. Shreve, a civil engineer, was diagnosed with learning disabilities at age 36. Many people will relate to his story of learning to drive whether they are the teacher or the student. This is an excerpt of an article published in the Learning Disabilities Association journal Newsbriefs *in May/June 1993. It is reprinted with permission.*

Left Brain/Right Brain Half Insane

by Nancy Edwards Clay

My left brain and my right brain
just don't get along.
My right brain makes decisions;
My left brain says they're wrong!
My left brain wants to clean the house;
my right brain says, "I'm bored!"
My left brain screams, "Be disciplined;
It cannot be ignored!"
My right brain says, "Be patient;
I've got a poem to write."
My left brain vows to nag, nag, nag,
and interferes for spite.
My left brain says, "Get organized!"
My right brain says, "I *can't*!"
My left brain says, "Try harder,
without so much complaint!"
If my right brain wins this inner war
our lives will be chaotic.
If my left brain wins this argument

I'll make us all psychotic!

(I'd structure us like generals

strictly regimented,

Organized and systemized

until we're all demented.)

This raging battle in my skull,

this inner stormy weather,

would clear up like a sunny day

if they'd just get together;

My right brain with my left brain,

in smooth cooperation,

So I could go about my life

free of hesitation.

For now, I brave the storm inside

and pray for peace in there

And hope I don't get so confused

I fail to brush my hair.

Nancy Edwards Clay, who has symptoms of attention deficit disorder, says she wrote this because "there is an argument going on in my head from sunrise to sunset, and even those wee hours of the morning when I can rarely sleep, anyway. Part of me is struggling to stay disciplined and organized and the other part of me is struggling to let my creative drives flourish. The part of me that yearns to be organized and structured is constantly being distracted and torn away from task by some creative idea that must be taken care of before it escapes into oblivion." This poem is copyrighted by the author and reprinted with her permission. Nancy lives in Oklahoma.

Nothing Succeeds Like Success

by Louise Fundenberg

Yes, there is life with learning disabilities. And NO, it doesn't go away with time—59 years! But you can't make it without help and understanding along the way. . . . Much of my help and understanding came from my family. From the very beginning, my mother taught me that "Nothing succeeds like success"—all I needed were a few good successes and I'd make it! I had outgrown my trike but could not balance a bike. (There were no training wheels in those days.) So . . . Santa brought me an Irish Mail. This is a wheeled cart upon which one sits. To make it go you pump the stick back and forth and steer with your feet. Boy, could I pump!

I wasn't very good at cutting but I did like paper dolls. I cut out some of these paper dolls one evening and then got ready for bed, having put my dress in the dirty clothes hamper. As Mother hung out the wash some days later, she found daylight coming through my dress where daylight did not belong. . . . Needless to say, I learned not to cut paper dolls on my lap.

World War II caused a change in our house that has given me a love of stories and words. I could not read but when "Granny" moved in I was one of the group of kids she read to. Being read to continued for me into my junior college days. It is not to be said I still couldn't read but I couldn't read fast enough. . . . Father read and talked history with me so it is his "B" grade as well as mine.

My parents provided tutors, teachers, and testers, looking for any and all ways to help me learn. The school also looked for some extra help for me because they could not understand how I could be "so dumb." After all, "Aren't you Eleanor and Bill's little sister? They were such good students in my class!"

and "Your twin sister, Martha, is doing just fine in Mrs. C's class." But I hated school so much I was late to school every day. Every afternoon I was taken out of my third grade class to go to Mrs. B, the kindergarten teacher, for help with reading! How embarrassing! At mid-year, it was decided that maybe I could learn better if I was placed in Mrs. C's class with my twin sister. I don't know if it helped or not. I am not even sure when I learned to read. I used to try to memorize the line that should be mine as we read around the "low" group. I could get away with it as long as the teacher went in order and there were pictures on each page. I would often get tripped up by using "Father" for "Daddy" or some word that gave the meaning of the story from the picture but was not on the page.

Spelling was, and still is, a nightmare. I did learn that some words had a "silent E." Most of my spelling words when written for the tests were the beginning and ending sounds with my old friend "silent E" thrown in for good measure. There weren't any middle sounds because I couldn't perceive them. With the "sound" advice "that everyone could learn to spell if they just studied," I tried to remember how the word looked and what letters were in it. Much of the time I would get nearly all the letters but they were never in the right order. . . . With the help of a tutor, I learned to trace my words with the pointer finger of the hand I write with. With words of many syllables, each syllable was written with a different color crayon. But I didn't find this tutor until I was going to junior college. The only reason I went to junior college was to complete my high school diploma. I had promised my mother I would get my diploma if she and Dad would let me out of high school. I dropped out of school in December of my senior year. I am amazed I had hung in there that long. In junior high, the counselor had told my mother I was not bright enough to go to college but she could not explain how "such a dummy" had scored 13th grade level in reasoning on the group test that had just been given to all the ninth graders.

In junior college I found friends and understanding as well as success. . . . I became active in women's sports and school service and I got good grades. I had support from my teachers. My English teacher really went to bat for me when the biology teacher stomped over to her office to let her know I had no right to be in school. I COULDN'T SPELL!! She pointed out to him that his job was to teach biology. If my answers were correct but misspelled, I should have credit. However, some battles are not always won. The biology teacher would not change his opinion. I was forced to drop the course.

Buoyed up by success I set out for the University of California, Santa Barbara, not understanding that the advisor there cared more for the research he was writing than about the classes he placed his students in. . . . At UCSB I started with just 12 units. But which 12! Zoology 1AB, Chemistry 1 and French 1. Now if you can't manage the sounds of your own native tongue, how can you learn a different one? But the "God of Education" said, "you are not educated until you have two years of a foreign language." I had to drop French and take an "F." When the help of a tutor, chemistry was passed with a "D." Zoology was a compromise. The teaching assistant in the lab didn't care how I spelled it. He told me that if he could understand what I meant and it was right I could have credit. The blue book tests in the lecture were not so forgiving. Once I tried to get the professor to let me bring in a new, clean, pocket dictionary so I could spell better than third grade words. He could see there were no notes in it but still it was not allowed. Thank God for my "A" in lab. One was not allowed a tape recorder either, so, although you listened very carefully, you could not get it all. I had learned a long time ago that, if I tried to take notes, I would tie up on spelling the words and lose what was being said. It was better never to miss class and connect what was said to what I had read. But I still missed some of the fine points.

I came to the University of California, Los Angeles, the

following year to begin a nursing major. But a congenital defect in my neck and back caused that balloon to break. I soon dropped out, not knowing what I wanted to do. I worked in the mail room at Cal Tech but I felt that I could do more with my life than pitch mail. I went back to school and finished college in Education. . . .

I have now retired, having taught for over 29 years. I've really enjoyed teaching and feel that I have helped many students in general education as well as special education who found learning difficult. Education was my niche.

Louise Fundenberg taught for 30 years in regular education and special education classrooms. She is president of the Orange County chapter of the Learning Disabilities Association of California. A version of this article originally appeared in the LDA-California newsletter, The Gram, *in August 1989 and is reprinted here with Louise's permission.*

Teacher, Teacher

by Richard Devine

Teacher, Teacher What do you see?

Can you see as far as Me?

Long school halls—closed doors!

Where could I go? Where could I turn?

You tried to force me to look through

your window but all I ever saw

was the sheer, blind rage within me,

Humiliation and anger

forced me to find myself

and not in the printed word.

Struggling with a book one day,

I said to myself, "Do it another way!"

And I succeeded.

Now you say I was a gifted child

Not so.

I simply never fit on your superhighway.

Were all the roads so wide

you couldn't help me find my trail?

Teacher, Teacher, I don't read,

I don't write. When I look

at a pile of books I fight!

This war lasted only a moment

for you but will last a lifetime for me.

You tried to bend me to fit

your jail of words— but I am free now,

and stand tall in my own way.

Richard Devine wrote this piece to show how he came to understand how he created his own method of learning and reporting. He uses this poem when he gives talks on dyslexia. He believes that reading and writing are only tools you use for learning—you learn by thinking. Richard Devine feels dyslexia is an advantage, not a disability. It has forced him to trust his own experience and understanding rather than rely on the experience of others. He is an accomplished goldsmith and the 1987 recipient of the Margaret Byrd Rawson Award, which is given annually to dyslexic adults who have overcome their learning disabilities to make significant accomplishments in their fields. This poem appeared in the spring/summer 1994 edition of dyslexia, the newsletter of the New York branch of the Orton Dyslexia Society. It is reprinted with his permission. Richard lives in New York.

How Our Parents Have Helped Us: Positive and Negative

by Gale L. Bell

As a member of ALDA (Association of Learning Disabled Adults) for the past two years, I realized how difficult it is to raise an LD child. The parents sense their child is different from other children but can't put their finger on what is the problem. A learning disability is invisible and is so foreign to the personal experience of the parent. They realize it takes their child much longer to accomplish what other children can do without effort. The parent feels helpless because he or she cannot help their child.

Many LD children are hyperactive, have a short attention span, and are in perpetual motion . . . some LD children are hypoactive. They withdraw from life, hardly moving, and are very slow to respond to anything.

The parents of an LD child quite often feel anger, frustration, guilt, pity and bitterness towards themselves, their friends and relatives, doctors, teachers, the whole school system and even their own child.

When the parents try to seek help and understanding for their LD child, they run into resistance from their doctors, teachers, and friends. Quite often these parents are accused of being over-protective and pushy. This leaves the parent fighting against the whole world. Frustration, defensiveness and self-doubt set in. . . .

The parents watch helplessly as their child slips further and further behind, each year adding new anguish. How frustrating and angry the parents feel to see their child agonize over reading, writing, arithmetic, and sports. Often their child is the brunt of his classmates' teasing, harassment, and cruelty.

. . .Quite often the child's responses to his peers are silly, immature and inappropriate.

I became very interested in this topic (and much more appreciative of *my* parents) when a young LD woman called me seeking help. It came out in our talk that her mother had never helped her—never read her assignments to her (she couldn't read) and never helped with her homework. I realized how much time and help my parents devoted to me and never complained or criticized.

The parents of those in ALDA have been very supportive. They have given much of their time, patience, strength, and love. Our parents have spent hours reading our assignments, helping with math and other homework, and taking us to doctors and tutors several times a week for years.

Many of our parents have worked hard to get learning disabilities recognized and understood in the school system, in the law, and in the public eye. It is our parents who helped start ACLD. . . .

These parents have sacrificed to get us special help and support in the school system. They have laid the foundation not only for us but for our children who might be LD. Some of our parents have battled so hard and for so long, they forgot that we are mature adults and the time has come for us to handle our own problems and life. They are blind to the fact that we must be responsible for ourselves. . . .

Parents have goals they set for their children. They want their children to be perfect, to do well in school and socially. It is very difficult for parents to accept the fact that their child will not come near those goals. The parents of LD children have to accept their child as he or she is, and this is very hard to do.

Parents see their child failing in school, failing socially, and having a hard time fitting into society. As their child grows older, the parents fear their child will not be able to support him or herself. In response, the parents become overprotective and don't let their child grow up. Many parents do everything for their LD child and demand nothing back except helplessness. They believe (or want to believe) their child is incapable of doing things for himself. Quite often parents do not demand that their LD child keep the commitments he or she has made. ALDA has a problem: Members volunteer to do certain jobs and then feel they are not responsible enough to do them.

Since quite often LD people mature more slowly than their peers, it is hard for a parent to know when to shift responsibility onto the shoulders of their child. . . .

As I said, it is not easy to be the parent of an LD child.

Gale Bell is an artist and a founding member of an organization for learning disabled adults now in its sixteenth year. She notes that her art expresses the "feelings (torments) of being learning disabled. I could quietly express myself without words and others could not tell what I was letting pour out through my hand and onto the paper." This essay was originally published in News- briefs, *the journal of the Learning Disabilities Association of America, and is reprinted here with permission. Gale lives in Maryland.*

How I See ADD

by Maryann Blust

I know when I do not understand a word or thought I always ask for examples. When the example is understood the light goes off and all the round pegs fall in the round holes and all the square pegs fall in the squares.

When ADD works to my advantage and in many cases it has, it is like a metropolitan orchestra that is playing in perfect harmony. All instruments playing alone and together as was intended by the composer. When it is at its worst, it is like having no conductor and everyone playing as they see fit or worse having no players. Just the instruments doing their own thing by themselves.

I never cared for magic or magicians. I always felt like everyone could see the sleight of hand except me and I was the only one on the outside looking in.

You see there are those blinks. "Hello," what just happened? Or the song verse, "We almost made it this time, didn't we?" All is going well and wham, all of a sudden you are lost and you have no idea why. Now I understand why. They are called blinks.

Maryann Blust has been diagnosed with ADD. Her philosophy is "You only fail if you do not try." She lives in Oklahoma.

The Fable of the Dragon Dyslexia

by Richard Bogia

I am Sir Richard, a brave, bold and daring Knight, in shining armor. I am always loyal to my King. My King has told me to defeat an evil dragon by the name of Dyslexia.

As I leave the great walls of the castle, I know where to find him. I must travel to the Forest of Reading. I know he is there because it's there that he causes the most harm.

As I get to the Forest of Reading I see the people of Wisdom boldly trying to defend the books of Knowledge. However, the dragon is stealing the books of Knowledge and burning the houses. My horse and I go to battle as I yell, "I'm Sir Richard the brave." Dyslexia replied with tongues of fire. The heat makes me mad. Now I have his full attention. An arrow pierces through the one hole in Dyslexia's armor. He drops the books of Knowledge and runs to his cave high in the mountains.

I tell the people of Wisdom that I will stay and help rebuild the houses. At last I return to the castle only to wonder, when will Dyslexia strike again?

I am Sir Richard, who with the King and the people of Wisdom, conquers Dyslexia.

Richard Bogia wrote this tale at age 27. He says, "Each of us comes into life with a package deal. Dyslexia is part of my package. I hope this short story will help people with their Dyslexia." This story originally appeared in the 1989 issue of Their World *magazine and is reprinted with permission.*

Learning to Dance

by Dale Brown

I was a learning disabled child who had difficulty in visual and auditory perception, knowing left from right, and motor coordination. This story will describe how it felt to learn to dance. I took the classes between the ages of seven and eleven, before my coping skills were well developed. Hopefully, the reader will gain a better understanding of what it's like to have this handicap, how it affects the emotions and relationships with other people.

What was dance class like? My father drove me to the studio. I'd enter the cool dressing room and change into my leotard. I loved its smooth feeling against my skin.

Then the class lined up. I stayed in the back to follow another student. The teacher led us in warm-up exercises. Music played. We sat down and spread our legs apart and bounced up and down. We knelt down and brought our arms around in a circle, like a windmill. We stood up and did a routine of kicks and bends and steps. It moved too fast for me, but I tried to do it.

Then we stood at the bar with our heels together and our toes out (first position). Then we'd "plee-ay," bending our knees as far as they'd go. We learned the other four ballet positions.

Sometimes, we'd sit in a circle and the teacher would beat a drum with random beats. We listened and tried to repeat the beats the way he did them. When the class did it together, I'd watch the student in front of me. When it was my turn, it was hard. I couldn't remember as many of the beats as the other students.

We did lots of exercises. The teacher didn't yell at me as often as most of my other teachers. He often said "very good." The problem was that he said "very good" to the other students more often than he said "very good" to me.

Sometimes, I talked back to the teacher. Once he told us to get into a ball and uncurl gracefully as if we were butterflies coming out of a cocoon. When he said I wasn't graceful, I told him that my science teacher said that butterflies came out of cocoons very slowly and sloppily and could hardly fly at first. Actually, I didn't really know what "graceful" meant. . . .

Sometimes, the teacher would say, "Dale, don't do that. Do this instead." He'd show me what I was doing wrong and then show me how to do it right. Why did he do the same thing both times? I couldn't understand it. Now, I know that I couldn't visually perceive the difference. But back then, I thought he was fooling me.

I took the beginner's class two years in a row. Then, in the intermediate class, I couldn't keep up. We learned a dance called "Greensleeves." I couldn't memorize the steps. I did fine while he taught us each step, but they wouldn't stay in my mind. We weren't learning in rows anymore, so I had to dance without anyone in front of me. I couldn't remember well enough to practice at home.

As a child, I had learned not to show emotion. I never cried, but always felt tears behind my eyes. Sometimes, in class, a few tears would squeeze out of the corners of my eyes. It released the pressure and felt very good, especially the coolness of the tears on my cheek. But I didn't want anyone to notice. Nobody said anything about it.

I was embarrassed so often, I was numb to feeling.

When I couldn't keep up with the intermediate class, they let me take the beginner's class again. I enjoyed it because the routine was comforting and finally, I could do many of the steps. But I felt ashamed of having taken it so many times and of being in class with younger children. . . .

The third time I took the class, I was allowed to perform in "Greensleeves" for a recital. I was excited. I remember wearing my costume and waiting my turn, afraid that I'd make a mistake. . . . Carefully, I walked out on tip toes, following the student in front of me. Then, all of us had to jump three times while "scissoring" our legs. Then we had to meet the other students and touch their hands across from them. Was I relieved when I met the right student! Then we went back to our original places and did more steps. Finally, the dance was over. I had not made any errors! I wanted to jump up and down and shout with joy, but I knew better.

I went behind the curtain of the dressing room to change my clothes.

"Dale did well," I heard someone say, "but she wasn't in rhythm to the music."

The happiness turned off, and again, I felt tears pressing hard against the corners of my eyes. I blinked hard to be sure they didn't creep out. I hadn't done it right after all.

How I needed a shoulder to cry on at that moment. I deserved to feel pride for overcoming a handicap that nobody knew I had. But the reality was that my performance was still significantly poorer than the other students. So, as usual, I was made to feel ashamed at a time which should have been one of triumph.

Behind the shame, there was anger. At that time, I couldn't feel it. But unconsciously, I knew that I should have been respected.

It is these strong emotions that lead many learning disabled boys to act out. However, as a little girl, this was not an option for me.

I'm glad that I took modern dance, though. The perceptual-motor training helped me. My dance teacher was more helpful than many of my other teachers. I'm not sure why or how, but I think he cared for me and tried to help me learn.

And caring helps learning disabled people most of all.

Dale Brown founded the Association of Learning Disabled Adults. Dale is the author of a manual called Steps to Independence for People with Learning Disabilities. *The above work is copyrighted in her name and reprinted with her permission. Dale lives in Washington, D.C. An example of her poetry appears in chapter 1.*

ADDvantages of ADD?

by Thomas Konczal

I am a 34-year-old adult with ADD. I have been on Ritalin for approximately 2 years and am doing fine. I am wondering if there are any others who feel that even though ADD makes some aspects of life difficult, ADD does have some tremendous advantages. Since being diagnosed and starting medication, I have become a "normal" person. Unfortunately, some qualities which gave me an advantage over the general population have disappeared.

I was always very intuitive and seemed to soak up information and stimuli like a sponge. I could be watching a TV show, listening to the radio, reading a book and overhearing a conversation with my wife and her friend and would be able to recall every detail of everything. Now, I seem to have "tunnel vision." I do my best when performing one task at a time.

In my pre-med era, I seemed to be running on instinct. I knew what to do and how to do it. I couldn't explain how I knew. I just knew. I think that being unfocused enabled me to pick up things that I now ignore. I have above average intelligence and have been able to compensate for some of the problems associated with ADD.

My main reason for seeking treatment was my inability to conform to social "rules." I cannot seem to pick up the subtle signals that other people unconsciously use. Consequently, I have been regarded as ignorant, rude, arrogant, cold, etc. Although I am doing great now, both personally and professionally, I somehow feel that being "normal" is . . . well . . . boring.

I used to be somewhat proud of the fact that my relatives and others thought I was different. If anyone had a problem, they would eventually ask me for advice because my point of view was usually very different from theirs and I would come up with some answers that never crossed their minds. Now, I feel like part of the herd, a sheep, baa, baa.

I keep thinking of that saying, "Be careful of what you wish for, you may receive it." Don't get me wrong, I'm not knocking normalcy. I'm just wondering if I was happier before or after?????

Thomas Konczal has discontinued his medication. He lives in Illinois.

LD

by Joan A. Levine, Ph.D.

My feet and my brain aren't quite the same
Though I can feel the beat, I can't repeat what I see
So I stand by the wall, confused and small;
Hiding my shame for not playing the game like the rest.

Bumping the doors, tables and drawers close to me.
No perception of the distance things are supposed to be.
Can't organize or integrate the information in my head
to communicate and participate, I look upon with dread.

Sometimes words don't make sense, I have no defense against a
        mysterious, undecipherable code,
That short circuits and misfires in desperation, perspires in
        ominous overload.
Wiggling in a chair, playing with my hair, my knuckles
        turning blue.
Can't hide the exaggerated motion, that makes such commotion
        and torments my body through.

I can tell you what it is and show you what it does—
But call it by its proper name, my head's a ball of fuzz.
Landmarks are important; a flagpole, sign or park
The directions North, South, East or West just leave me in
        the dark.

Balancing a checkbook or tipping the right change,
Even after months of practice becomes a chore that's strange.
Behaving in each situation in an appropriate way
is worse than capers, anchovies and jogging every day.

New ways of doing things, learning strategies I was taught
To help improve a lot of skills and unravel what I thought.
When I grew up I thought I'd find a special space
in a world without a struggle, I'd really have a place.

But people never listen, they don't care if you get stuck.
They judge by how you act and how you make a buck.
Learning disabilities never seem to quit.
They plague you all your life and never let you fit.

Joan Levine wrote this to express her frustration as a person who looks quite "normal" but who has the "hidden handicap" of perceptual and language disorders. This poem originally appeared in the May/June 1994 issue of The Gram, *the newsletter of the Learning Disabilities Association of California, and is reprinted with Dr. Levine's permission.*

Chapter 4

Challenging Voices

The writings in this chapter are the ones that truly challenge us. They force us to rethink all of the stereotypes and labels ever used to describe individuals with learning problems. They emphasize the unique qualities of all people and extend that "uniqueness" to the people whom we call special.

In chapter 1, "Children's Voices," we saw how even the youngest child understands his or her learning disability and works hard to be accepted in spite of learning difficulties. Chapter 2, "Young Adult Voices," carries that thought of acceptance even further. These individuals did not always feel that they were different. In fact, they felt that acceptance—socially, emotionally, educationally, and vocationally—should be automatic.

Chapter 4 reaffirms the abilities of individuals who are regarded as having disabilities. These people have taken their special qualities and used them to further their education and to make significant contributions to society. Most of the contributors here are also represented in other chapters. They have written about their disabilities and their journeys. Their writings show that they are defined not only by their learning disabilities, but also by their unique talents and gifts, which they are eager to display. The authors in this chapter demonstrate that everyone has the capacity to be creative, regardless of learning ability, and that creativity is often propelled and enhanced by difficult life experiences. As contributor Jessica Lenz puts it, "It's not what a person looks like that makes a person. It's what's to be shared inside that is a gift one cannot replace." The works that follow are a source of inspiration to parents and children living with learning disabilities.

A Seagull

by Kara Chrzescyanek

A seagull flies high in the sky

Why can't I?

Someday I will find out why.

This short poem was originally published in Their World *magazine, 1983, and is reprinted here with permission.*

Books! Books! Books!

by Phillip Russell

Books! Books! Books!
They never lose their looks.
They always take the blame.
They always have a name.
Books! Books! Books!

You read 'em in teeny tiny nooks
You find 'em in libraries.
There's books about scary Harrys,
Or books about poems and homes,
Or books about cones and bones.

Books! Books! Books!
There's books about hooks,
And books about crooks,
And books about looks.
Read funny books.
Books! Books! Books!

Phillip Russell wrote this at age 11 while attending the Crossroads School. He lives in Pennsylvania.

I Am a Rock

by Andrea Rose Schneider

I am a rock
    —a Geode to be exact
I am always evolving:

Solid at first glance.
    —of round configuration or slightly oblong.
but from the start, in my center,
    —it's glistening with an array of minerals and water.
A combination of atoms, linked together in patterns.

Then intense heat and pressure is exerted;
    —I am molding and transforming my appearance
In my core.

Time passes . . . rolling through life;
I am still rough and coarse,
    —but, if split in two mirroring halves,
one sees all my treasures:
Lines and circular waves of white and gray—an Agate mass.
On top, I stick-out
    —in beautiful, long, crystalline shapes.
Half colored rose and half opaque.

Andrea Rose Schneider is a graduate student in Boston University's Learning Support Services program. She is an artist who works in applied arts as well as computer art. She is from New York.

Melodic Logic

by Kate Shannon

I play my piano
    as the rain falls.
Playing my piano is like the rain
    tapping on my roof and walls.

I love the pitter patter,
    just like pressing on my piano keys.
At times the piano frustrates me
    but the rain puts me at ease.

I try to memorize a piece or two.
    When I hear the rain,
I try to concentrate,
    but gaze off through the window pane.

Rain has an even beat,
    I can almost count the drops.
When it is raining less and less,
    I almost know when the rain will stop.

Rain is a continuing motion,
    rain falls one drop by one.
In a few hours,
    what I will find is the sun.

Kate Shannon is a graduate of the Threshold Program at Lesley College. She lives in Maryland.

The Twig

by Jesse W. Adcox

The chill wind bites deeply into the trees, turning their sap to ice. Jagged peaks reach to the sky like the stabbing fingers of a giant, making me feel small and insignificant. As the wind races through the trees it knocks over anything that isn't rooted down. Snow, falling like millions of miniature shooting stars, pelts the ground, piling layer upon layer, covering almost all the forest. The wind howls as it buffets the branches, leaves, and twigs.

One twig in particular catches my eye, seemingly indifferent to the elements. Frozen there like the paw of a wolf breaking through the snow, it does not move. Almost ten inches of it are visible above the snow. It's a piece from a White Pine tree, one of hundreds in this forest, with its needles twisted and bent slightly. To the touch they are smooth and brittle, splintering in my hand. The twig is shiny, coated in ice. Yet I still get the impression that it is alive, stopped in time, waiting for the healing rays of the sun to shatter its icy prison. This thing that at a touch, would crumble to nothingness, holds so much energy.

Jesse Adcox wrote this while attending Landmark College in Vermont. A poem by Jesse appears in chapter 2.

Mandy Michelle Misty Moore

by Denise Eggleston

Mandy Michelle Misty Moore

Wouldn't clean the kitchen floor.

Vacuuming wasn't a thrill to her.

She'd rather run and play for sure.

Sweeping was much too boring to do

And she wouldn't mop up any sticky goo.

So she left it exactly how it was

And ignored her chores . . . just because!

She had other things on her mind

No matter she hadn't a place to dine.

The floor was filled with tracked in mud

And sewage treatment from a flood.

Trash from wrappers, boxes and cans,

Taxes, bills and rubberbands,

Leftover food even the dog wouldn't smell,

Banana peels and stinky bug repel,

Stains from coffee on the drawers

Filled with fruit pits and apple cores.

And you'd think after seeing this horror

That Mandy would clean up the floor.

Right? Wrong!

She closed up the kitchen filled with junk

And even though the whole house stunk,

She left it how it was until

Guests were coming! No time to kill!

She cleaned, swept, sponged and broomed

Until finally she cleaned up the room.

Things worked out for Mandy . . . this time!

So I guess there's no moral to this rhyme.

Denise Eggleston wrote this at age 13. She has been diagnosed with atten-tion deficit disorder (ADD). Her mother, Nancy, has written a poem which appears in chapter 5. They live in California.

I Am Somebody

by Kimberly Harter-Key

I Am Somebody

I am neither great nor small,
But I must remember myself
As an equally important person.

I must strive for my goals,
No matter how unreachable they appear.

I must venture about my future,
With new heights to my confidence.

I must be my own person,
And not look for others
Who I can compete with.

I must view myself as a success
And not worry about how other people view
me.

I must peer across an endless, blue ocean

At the dazzling sunset,

And say to the world

That I will contribute my share of good fortune.

I must walk the shore in the morning sunrise

And wonder what will happen the next day.

My life is neither great nor small.

I am just somebody.

Kimberly Harter-Key is a graduate of the Threshold Program at Lesley College. An essay by Kimberly appears in chapter 2. She lives in Massachusetts.

On the Hill with Spirits

by Scott M. Martin

every time I look at a landscape
I see things others do not
I see the spirits of the land
they sit in the pines
that sway in the wind
as though the waves of an ocean roll in
or on a hill watching such as I
no motion but the eyes scanning
like an owl to observe
every detail of the land
as the December air
storms down my spine
a tree creaks
as it talks to me
I reply with a wild howl
which emerges from my soul
I wonder
was I ever an Indian

Scott Martin is a student at the Kildonan School. This poem won first place in the upper school division of the Kildonan literature department's creative writing contest. Scott has written about his learning disability in a poem appearing in chapter 1. He lives in New Jersey.

Untitled

by Amy Smith

Blackness like a moonless winters sky
that fills my head with dizzy anticipation

Brutality, injustice, pain and horror that
our forefathers escaped from to this unknowing nation

Brothers and sisters in our violent society, fight
back in the name of pride and greed—money and power,

Death stains our chaotic city streets, scarlet red,
hour after hour,

There's no place to go, there's nowhere to
play,

A bloody trail trickles where bodies
may lay,

Mayhem runs rampant through our
black, hardened hearts,

The grievance of a young child's eulogy
hangs in my memory like a work of art.

I am no longer an innocent bystander in
this troubled world of pure insanity.

Propaganda and the media plague all of
humanity.

Hallucinations of how things could be, haunt
my soul and my mind.

Too many unfortunate matters complicate
the ordinary everyday grind.

All respect is lost in the heart of
the stereotypical suburban youth.

It's time the yuppy generation got off their
car phones and paid attention to the blatant Truth.

I sit back and watch our reckless behavior,
trusting myself, never trusting others

Seeing stupidity and ignorance
destroying my sisters and brothers.

Amy Smith wrote this at age 16. She has attention deficit disorder and auditory memory problems. She lives in California.

We the People

by Jessica Lenz

We the people are art.

Art like music has harmony.

We create enhanced beauty,

creating harmony between cultures,

religion and races.

We the people are art,

with different sculptured features,

no one, more beautiful than the other.

We walk with pride.

We the people are art,

and art like music has harmony.

Jessica Lenz is a graduate of the Threshold Program at Lesley College. Jessica has written about her challenges in a poem appearing in chapter 2. She lives in Massachusetts.

One Word

by Avi Ostchega

There is a word in the English language, and indeed in all languages, a word that is the name for one of our strongest emotions.

It is a word that has taken form in many different ways.

To some it is an incurable plague, to others it is the motivation for acts that otherwise would not be possible.

In some parts of the world it is born with the rise of the sun every day. In others it is only a shadow echoing in our foot steps.

Only know this . . . wherever man is, and will be, it will be there with him.

It comes to man's side in as many different ways as stars in the cold black sky. It comes with an icy touch on man's shoulder as he sleeps. It comes in the red panic of man struck in the face by life, trapped in his own mortality. It is with man from the time of his first entrance to the time of his last exit.

When man is weak it can control him, its evil demon ripping into man's soul with razor sharp talons.

It can help men who tower strong and cruel over the weak and helpless as they themselves cower deep in their own souls, clutching to the hate and pain as a child clutches the mother's breast.

For the man who is truly strong it is but one fiber in the power he holds, a fiber to be respected and awed so that it might only be made to serve him.

It is not a fair beast for it does not see the face on which it strikes, nor does it care.

It is unfeeling as the bullet, not knowing whom it topples or whom it spares.

Those who claim not to know the beast, know it best.

Man himself is in love with it, having had the burning romance for centuries.

In the realm of the emotions it sheds the darkness so that man may see the light.

It is a lone creature clamping masses, sometimes whole populations of man's world, in iron fists.

As with any evil, and it is the purest evil, it has servants . . . servants in all times. It was these servants that rode as the horsemen in the burning shadow of the twisted cross.

However, let men not think it all powerful; it cannot be without man, and men who will serve it.

As the black of night is pierced and at last overcome by the light of day, the beast too is chased from man's soul . . . back to the depths it had risen from, there to sleep until the marching of old weathered time passes. Once again to become only a resonating sound. To be uttered by the mouth of man at every corner of his world as he pays ignorant tribute to a universal demon lurking behind one four-letter word . . . fear.

Avi Ostchega is a student at Montgomery College. He states that he has "only recently unlocked the abilities and passage past frustration which has allowed me to begin to finally make positive progress in the scholastic environment." He lives in Maryland.

Exploring New Beginnings

by Elizabeth Lord

If I went to Asia.

    to find a tiger or a bear

it would be a beginning

    of traveling here to there.

If I went to Egypt.

    I'd see the King Tut's bed.

of sparkling jewels and diamonds,

    gleaming o'er his head.

If I went to China.

    to claim a panda rare.

I'd let you come and see him.

    and feel his furry hair.

If I went to England.

    I'd meet the lovely Queen

and spending the day with her,

    would simply be a dream.

If I sailed to Ancient Rome.

played in the Olympics and won,

and got a golden trophy

it would nearly weigh a ton.

I'd like to travel round the world.

I would go any time.

but my parents won't allow it.

you see, I'm only nine.

Elizabeth Lord created this poem in 30 minutes and spent 60 minutes copying it over due to her dysgraphia. It was originally published in Their World *magazine, 1993, and is reprinted with permission.*

Friendship

A Collaborative Poem

Friendship is like a roller coaster

It has its ups and downs.

Like the waves, it comes in and out.

Like rolling rapids, it sometimes moves quickly with bumps,

yet sometimes is smooth.

Like an echo, it goes back and forth.

Friendship like a grade, cannot be bought but must be earned.

Like a balloon, it can grow bigger and bigger,

but like a chicken in the oven, when it's done, it's done.

Friendship can be like a newborn colt.

It can start off weak, unable to stand, and end up on strong legs.

Like a diamond, it can sparkle or be dull.

Friendship is like a ticking clock.

It looks toward the future and not the past.

Like a shooting star, it bursts forth with flashing colors.

Life

A Collaborative Poem

Life is like a tree.

It starts out small and goes through changes,

Creating fruits, it grows and it dies.

Like a seesaw,

Is full of ups and downs.

Like a fountain,

It can burst forth refreshingly,

Or like old cherries,

Life can dry up and turn bitter.

Life is like a tornado or a washing machine,

Moves in rapid cycles,

Like trying to diet,

It is a never ending struggle.

Life like music,

Flows,

Like an open sea,

It lasts forever, always changing.

These two poems were collaborative efforts by creative writing classes led by the late Janet Senzer, assistant director of the Threshold Program at Lesley College.

Chapter 5

Family Voices

It is often harder to watch someone you love deal with a disability than to experience the disability firsthand. The ways in which parents and other family members deal with this reality are varied.

On the following pages are writings by parents, grandparents, sisters, and brothers that demonstrate how they have learned to cope with having a family member with a learning disability. Love is the common thread that binds their works, the determination that their loved one ultimately will be appreciated for his or her strengths and not penalized for his or her weaknesses. Some of the family members contributing to this chapter also have learning disabilities.

These essays and poems are a guide for emotional survival. The realization that other families have survived what you may be experiencing can provide tremendous relief. As we saw in chapter 3, learning disabilities and attention deficits do not disappear. Families as well as the individual with the learning disability learn to compensate and structure situations so that the problem does not become overwhelming.

The contributors come from families coping with a wide variety of disabilities. Their loved ones may have learning disabilities, attention deficit disorder, or Down syndrome. But the actual diagnoses do not matter; what does matter is that each of these individuals has special learning needs. The families share similar experiences. Their loved ones do not learn or behave in pre-dictable ways. The disabilities can cause confusion and frustration and create stress and turmoil. They can also bring love, humor, and comfort.

The road is rocky, and family members need encouragement and praise as well for their struggles and accommodations. We need to acknowledge the fact that their lives are often made more difficult due to the disability of their child, grandchild, sister, or brother. They need friends who are understanding and not judg-mental. They don't need to be made to feel guilty for having their moments of anger.

The family members who have contributed to this book have felt a need to share their experiences with others in the hopes that they might help someone else get through the unexpected. This act of sharing also helps them feel less alone. They show how to uncover the "specialness" in each child and how to celebrate his or her unique qualities. They acknowledge the difficulty of life with a child with special needs and have turned that difficulty into a challenge that forges a path for others to follow. Their under-standing and tolerance did not come without great effort and tears. As one parent states, "He never knew about the tears shed out of sight by a very concerned mother." These voices echo the feelings and hopes of many families and let them know they are not alone.

Bedtime Wishes

by Mary Daum

It's getting late, it's time for bed.

My nerves are frazzled—my eyes are red

from tears and heartbreak—sometimes I weep

for the little boy who is fast asleep.

I creep into his room and see

a sleeping angel who looks like me.

His blonde curls circle his cute little head.

He looks so tiny as he sleeps in his bed.

He's a beautiful child, but the light is so dim

His thumb's in his mouth, it comforts him

As I watch him, so quiet and still

Love wells up inside me, and it always will.

I wish I could take all his sadness away

and help him to have a happy day.

A day when he could have lots of friends

A day full of happiness that never ends.

I wish that he could have a day
When he could laugh and run and play
by the rules of all those children's games.
Then no one would call him those hurtful names.

I wish for a day when he wasn't alone
because a parent had sent him home
for misbehaving and getting too wild.
I wish I could help my little child.

As I lean down to kiss his sweet face
I say a short prayer and ask for the grace
to help him through another day.
We'll conquer his ADD, we'll find a way.

Mary Daum wrote this about her son, who has attention deficit disorder(ADD). She published it in 1994 in her newsletter, ADD-ONS. She lives in Illinois.

What Is a Learning Disability?

by Belva Barnhardt

It's eighteen years. . . .

Eighteen years, this month, that I have lived with a child who has learning disabilities.

At first, it's holding a beautiful healthy baby in your arms and having all of the hopes and dreams for a rich and blessed life for him.

It's waiting for the nurse to bring a seven-month-old baby from the recovery room after an accident which demanded the attention of a neurosurgeon.

It's sitting in a doctor's office and asking, "Why? Why does he have such severe falls for no reason? Four black eyes in two years cannot be normal!"

It's seeing a two-year-old toddle across the yard, pick a flower, and delightedly hold it up for Grandma to smell.

It's watching a kindergarten student show embarrassment because he "hasn't learned his colors."

It's watching a five-year-old sit with his Dad and learn all of the moves on the chessboard.

It is not understanding why he cried suddenly about going to the special summer program at school.

It's the agony of being told several years later that Mrs. __ made him stay in the closet at school because "I was bad."

It's watching a pre-schooler willingly reach up to grasp the neck of an old orderly who has come to take him to the operating room.

It's pleading with a principal, "He desperately needs another year in the first grade."

It's going to school four weeks into the second year and hearing, "You were right. He can't handle second grade at all.

We made a mistake. We'll move him back. You may select the teacher."

It's struggling for answers, understanding. Always, why? Why can't he learn?

It's knowing something is terribly wrong, hearing a teacher say, "He'll grow out of it," and knowing for sure that he won't.

It's feeling frustrated and uncertain myself, saying unthinkingly, "Do you think you'll go to college?" and hearing, "I just want to get through second grade!'

It's seeing a surprised and loving teacher lean down to hug a youngster she thought had left, and watching then a "buddy" say good-bye once again with a hug.

It's praying, hoping and then hearing a psychologist say, "Your child is mentally retarded."

It's knowing you can, deep inside yourself, accept this, but remembering that five-year-old playing chess.

It's hearing again, "We were wrong. He tests borderline on I.Q. tests, but knocks the top out of the non-verbal reasoning test."

It's asking, "What now?" and hearing, "There are no services for your child in this school system nor any nearby."

It's camping at the beach after a tidal wave had been publicized, listening to the waves pounding against the shore, and hearing a quiet voice in the dark ask, "Daddy, is that one of those Tiger Waves?"

It's hoping, ever searching . . . physicals, blood tests, psychologicals, and finally hearing a concerned professional say, "Do you know about. . . ? There is a Division for Disorders of Development and Learning."

It's agonizing over page after page of questionnaires— When did your child first draw a circle? Log everything your child eats for two weeks.

It's spending three whole days with competent professionals who delve into every facet of your family's lives.

It's hearing, while waiting for the EEG, "No, I'm not afraid, but my stomach is," and silently blessing a Dad who responds, "Well, I think that's called bravery."

It's hearing a renowned pediatrician/psychiatrist say, "This is best described as a genetic mistake. His brain just does not process information in the same way ours does. He is of average intelligence and can learn, but information will have to be channeled into the brain in different ways."

It's coming home and giving thanks for the teacher who meets with the staff of the evaluation team and says, "There are others who need a different approach, and we can. . . ."

It's driving over 100 miles two days each week while taking an overload in summer school, to make sure he has the benefit of speech therapy in the summer.

It's being met at the door late one afternoon with a report card showing the dreaded D and hearing the words, "But David says at least it's passing."

It's watching the kindness of children when he doesn't understand or the game doesn't go just right.

It's sitting up until midnight trying to help a seventh grader who has been "tracked" cope with being tormented by students whose problems are more severe than his.

It's overhearing another student say to him, "You sure do talk funny."

It's giving thanks for an L.D. resource teacher who provides encouragement and a respite from agonizing hours in class when he is told over and over, "You just don't try."

It's sitting with a group of co-workers, hearing the comment, "There's no such thing as learning disabilities," and thinking how fortunate that person is to have perfect, capable, and healthy children.

It's watching a young man pore over a driver's manual preparing for the test, and seeing him pass with flying colors.

It's going every quarter for a conference with new teachers and hearing many say, "I just wasn't aware there was a problem. He is so well behaved in class," and knowing that it's that "acceptable" behavior which has probably saved him.

It's sharing his pleasure over the A in math that he has earned and not worrying about the D in another subject where 50% of your grade is based on classroom behavior.

It's having to send him to the grocery store for the third time to correct the mistake he made the first time, knowing all the time it would have been much simpler to have gone myself.

It's wondering, worrying, feeling overwhelmed and pessimistic about his future.

It's knowing he will deal with this disability every day he lives, and yet feeling elated and optimistic that the future does hold for him all the hopes and dreams I envisioned eighteen years ago.

It's thanking God for blessing the lives in our family with his presence. Perhaps it is only through our love and understanding of him that we learn to be patient with others.

Belva Barnhardt wrote the above for the 1979 edition of Chalk Talk, *the newsletter of the Dalton, Georgia, school district, where she is director of special education. The essay is about her son, Mark, who is now out of school, married, and employed as a draftsman. It is reprinted with her permission.*

Small Blessings

by Rosalie Marie Bolenbaugh Baker

The little girl came to my lap, one day;
her hair was long, golden and tousled from play.

Her smile was bright, her eyes shown blue;
and her face glowed, when she looked at you.

She was bouncy and happy, as we all should be;
and when she laughed, it tickled me.

She climbed on my knee, and gave me a kiss;
'Twas a blessing from heaven, that I couldn't miss.

The pleasures in life, surely abound;
hidden here, there and always around.

Look to your left and then to your right;
look at the day and into the night.

Can you see the blessings, shining through?
I wondered, what happened to me and you.

For one small child, could bring such bliss;

by her bright smile and one wee kiss.

Happiness seek, wherever you go;

for you see, this child, "was slow."

She never could hurt or cause pain;

her love is true and never vain.

If we were more like this child, day by day;

We'd help each other, along life's way.

Rosalie Baker wrote this poem about her new stepgranddaughter. Rosalie lives in Florida.

Untitled

by Lindsey Gaines

Hi, my name is Lindsey. I am 10 and my sister is 13. She is in special classes in school because she can't read or do math or write good. Sometimes I hate her because she always yells and screams and fights with me. Most of the time mom helps her and there is no time to help me. I really love her even if she yells because she lets me sleep in her room when I don't want to sleep in mine and she loves me a lot. Mom says she is really kind and loving and really gets mad at herself not me. I can't wait for her to go to sleep away camp but when she goes I always miss her very much. I help her with her homework when no one knows.

Lindsey Gaines composed this about her sister Jessica, who has learning disabilities and attention deficit disorder. They live in New Jersey.

The Little Glass Girl

by Nancy Edwards Clay

I have a little glass girl.
Her heart and soul
are more fragile
than the hearts and souls
of others.

The smallest things shatter her,
and the jagged fragments
of her heart
tear into the souls of anyone close;
anyone, who dares to love her.

Loving her is a risk;
the pain of caring
is almost too great
to bear.

This world was not made
for little glass girls.
This world laughs at those
who break too easily . . .
It jostles and shoves them
so that it can boast
of its own invulnerability.

My little glass girl
teases and taunts the world.
She defies it.
And it turns and lashes out against her,
damning her
for being
a little glass girl.

I am here to pick up the pieces
and glue her shattered soul back together
until that day
when she either becomes strong
or is hopelessly broken.

God help us.

Look at her.
In the sunlight she sparkles
more beautifully than any.
That must be the light of hope.

Nancy Edwards Clay wrote this in 1985 to describe the way she felt many times as the mother of a daughter with emotional and mental problems. This poem is copyrighted by Nancy Edwards Clay and reprinted with her permission. She writes about her own disability in chapter 3. Nancy and her daughter live in Oklahoma.

Welcome to Holland

by Emily Perl Kingsley

I am often asked to describe the experience of raising a child with a disability—to try to help people who have not already shared that unique experience to understand it, to imagine how it would feel. It's like this. . . .

When you're going to have a baby, it's like planning a fabulous vacation trip—to Italy. You buy a bunch of guide books and make your wonderful plans. The Coliseum. The Michelangelo David. The Gondolas in Venice. You may learn some handy phrases in Italian. It's all very exciting.

After months of eager anticipation, the day finally arrives. You pack your bags and off you go. Several hours later, the plane lands. The stewardess comes in and says, "Welcome to Holland."

"HOLLAND?!?" you say. "What do you mean Holland? I signed up for Italy! I'm supposed to be in Italy. All my life I've dreamed of going to Italy."

But there's been a change in the flight plan. They've landed in Holland and there you must stay.

The important thing is that they haven't taken you to a horrible, disgusting, filthy place, full of pestilence, famine, and disease. It's just a different place.

So, you must go out and buy new guide books. And you must learn a whole new language. And you will meet a whole new group of people you would never have met.

It's just a <u>different</u> place. It's slower-paced than Italy, less flashy than Italy. But after you've been there for a while and you catch your breath, you look around . . . and you begin to notice that Holland has windmills . . . and Holland has tulips. Holland even has Rembrandts.

But everyone you know is busy coming and going from

Italy . . . and they're all bragging about what a wonderful time they had there. And for the rest of your life, you will say, "Yes, that's where I was supposed to go. That's what I had planned."

And the pain of that will never, ever,ever, ever go away . . . because the loss of that dream is a very, very significant loss.

But . . . if you spend your life mourning the fact that you didn't get to Italy, you may never be free to enjoy the very special, the very lovely things . . . about Holland.

Emily Perl Kingsley is the parent of a child with special needs. The idea for this story came to her while she was counseling a new mother of a child with Down syndrome. It was later incorporated into the CBS Movie of the Week "Kids Like These." © 1987 by Emily Perl Kingsley and reprinted with permission of the author. All rights reserved. Emily lives in New York.

Someone Please Hear My Cry

by Jean Carlson

Here I am a child who's eight

   Does someone care about my fate?

Where will I be when I turn nine?

   To others will it still seem that I'm fine?

Perhaps there will be just one who'll see

   how important learning really is to me.

I reverse letters and words when I write.

   My spelling is terrible, it's part of my plight.

Months of the year are easy to repeat,

   but in my life they bring defeat.

I want to read more than I'm able.

   I'd like to enjoy reading a fable.

At one time I'm told so many things to do.

   It's fantastic for me if I remember two.

My books and shoes are hard to find.

   Why is it I forget where they are all the time?

Don't bruise me more by saying I'm just slow,

   In my limited ways I work hard, for I too want to glow.

I need help and much understanding

   and with it I won't be so demanding.

Why won't you see my problems are real?

   Am I a threat to you in all that you feel?

Some days your attitude makes me ashamed.

   I don't understand, am I to blame?

I have special needs unlike most others.

   Why won't you listen to my mother?

You're the adults, the leaders, I thought.

   Why do my problems have to be fought?

There are ways to help me, so I am told.

   PLEASE, Oh Please, hear my cry before I'm too old.

Jean Carlson is the parent of a son with learning disabilities. This poem origi-nally appeared in the 1989 issue of Their World *magazine. It is reprinted with permission.*

Letting Go

by Brenda Harris

I always knew that my son's first day of school would be a big day for me, too. Other milestones like his first smile and first step caught me unaware. But this time I would be ready. I was all set to record the symbolic end to his early childhood years with the videocamera, waiting by the front door.

The big day is here at last. David has new clothes, a new backpack, and a new smile. He can hardly contain himself. Finally he will join the "big kids" on the bus ride to school. He is looking forward to meeting his teachers and classmates. I hope I have prepared him well for this important new adventure.

As he's ready to step into his future, I find myself lingering in the past. I remember well those first years of David's life when I found myself unwillingly immersed in the inevitable chaos of life with a small child. And my small child had a disability (probably Tourette syndrome with characteristics of ADD and PDD, also). Sometimes, during a particularly bad day, I looked longingly as the familiar yellow school bus picked up the neighborhood children. I looked forward to having a school-aged child. Oh, the things I would do with my free hours when David was in school! I would read novels, write, exercise, shop, organize the house, and maybe even get a part-time job.

But, as David grew and changed, so did the pattern of our lives together. Around age 4 he calmed down quite a bit. Our busy days together included library storytimes, gym classes, and trips to parks, pools and malls. There was lots of time for playing, laughing, reading, and hugging. I enjoyed the special bond between us, a bond forged by our time together.

Here comes the bus, brakes squealing as it rounds the

corner. I hug David tightly, and hold him close for just a moment longer. I position the videocamera as he eagerly climbs the bus steps. I get a perfect shot as he turns to give me one last excited wave. As the bus pulls away I see his face pressed against the window. I am glad that he is still smiling.

As I stand alone at the corner, waving until the bus is out of sight, I reflect on how hard this leavetaking has been for me. I am aware that never again will our days be so totally intertwined, our lives so comfortably connected. From now on large blocks of David's waking hours will be spent away from me. I won't be able to protect him from the taunting and teasing that he is often on the receiving end of because he's a little different. Although the intellectual part of me knows that he has to begin to make his own way, the mom part of me wishes I could protect him always. He will be meeting people and experiencing things apart from me. I will only know the parts of his day that he chooses to reveal to me.

As I turn away and walk back home, I realize how this is a day of beginnings for both of us. It is David's first day of formal education and the first of many lessons for me in learning to let go.

Brenda Harris's son was diagnosed with pervasive developmental disorder in 1990. He is in regular third-grade classes with special education services. Brenda and her son live in Virginia.

Voices Through the Bedroom Walls

by Noreen Boyle

Again tonight I hear my brother's voice carrying out a conversation—sometimes playing the part of two people, at other times just one.

When we were younger, in the same setting—he in his bedroom and me in mine—I would hear him through my bedroom wall and would yell out, "Who's in there with you?" And he would stop his talking and yell back, "Nobody."

"Then stop talking to yourself." For a few minutes there would be quiet. But gradually and inexorably, I'd hear his voice again, at first muffled by his pillow, but as his conversation would grow more intense, the volume would slowly increase.

Eventually, I began to realize that this was his way of getting through his days and gathering up the courage to face tomorrow. He was rewriting a script in which he didn't like the way his character was portrayed. This way his character could fight back against the bully, charm the heroine or score the winning run.

Noreen Boyle wrote this entry in her journal after she returned home from her first semester of college. She says, "The understanding I gradually gained while growing up with Michael perhaps pointed me toward the various para-professional summer jobs I held. . . . In any event, it certainly prepared me to better understand their needs and frustrations." She is now a registered nurse living in New York.

And every night I'd listen to him rewriting and then rehearsing the revised script. But on the following day, never did he win the battle, the girl or the game. Too many in the cast of his daytime play were ignorant and insensitive actors. But for a few minutes in his darkened bedroom, he held the spotlight and had his chance to shine.

Again tonight I hear his voice through the walls. But tonight I don't interrupt—I let him change the ending of his daily nightmare if only for a few minutes so that he can face the sun the following morning.

Help for Parents

by Susan Lunden

As a parent of a child involved in special education, I would like to inform other parents that there is support and help for you and your child. I too never got involved in the monthly Parent Advisory Council meetings because I didn't fully understand what they were all about. But finally, after years of frustration, I needed to find support to get some changes for my daughter's education.

I attended my first meeting and found support and guidance from other parents "who have been there," or are going through similar issues. I received phone numbers, names, and other resources that could help me.

I found out that my daughter has legal rights to her education and that I have a choice to go as far as the court system if need be.

There are approximately 1800 students involved in Special Education in my town. At most PAC meetings there are a handful of parents. Recently at a workshop for parents and educators on the topic of Integration of Our Schools, there were again too few parents. Why?

Probably, like me they didn't know if they belonged there, or if they would understand what was being talked about.

Susan Lunden wrote this as a letter to the editor of the Daily Evening Item, *Lynn, Massachusetts, and it was reprinted in the April 1991 issue of* NewsLine, *published by the Federation for Children with Special Needs. It is reprinted with permission from NewsLine. Susan lives in Massachusetts.*

Maybe they didn't feel they had a right to ask for more or better for their child. Each and every one of those 1800 students deserves and has a legal right to the highest quality education possible.

We as parents are our children's best advocates. We know better than anyone else what is best for them and what works.

The power of parents together is what creates change. Get involved. Get the support for yourself and you, child. You deserve it and have a right to it as well.

The Autism Book

by Chris Ferrino

Hi, my name is Chris Ferrino. I am going to teach you about autism. You are born with it. I have a brother with it. It is scary and it is sad.

Some people laugh at him. Would you?

He knows how to talk a little. He knows how to say his abc's and 123's. It is fun to teach Vincent. I love my brother.

Autism is a lot of things. It is some people who do not know how to talk, or someone who hates bright light.

The End

Chris Ferrino composed this in second grade to help explain his brother's autism to his friends. He dedicated it to his brother, Vincent. They live in Massachusetts.

From a Mother to Her Son

by Laura Bulger

This isn't fair!
I give up!
I don't care!

The tears streak down
your cheeks, so red
You sob and hold
your head

All the while as you are crying
You tell yourself
"Just keep trying."

The pages blur
All into one.
This work, it seems
Will never get done.

Mom, please help me
I can't think straight
Is this supposed to be
My fate?
Will all my days seem so long?
Will all my work be marked wrong?

Just dry your tears
Breathe in deep, let it go
I'll sit next to you
We'll take it slow.

Little by little
to your surprise,
Right before your bleary eyes,
You see the work it's getting done!
Your confusion you've overcome!

Just take it easy
Take it slow
The days may seem long
Your work may seem wrong
But in the end you will see—
Your fate will change,
You will be strong!

These times will pass
And fade to grey.
These memories of you and
Your mom will bring comfort someday.
When your work gets hard
And the pages blur
Remember, my special one—
The days aren't long
Your work was seldom wrong
But best of all
Now you are strong.

This poem originally appeared in the 1992 issue of Their World *magazine and is reprinted with permission.*

Bundles of Gifts

by Janet Vohs

Recognizing and celebrating the gifts of another are among the most rare and precious gifts we can give. Many of us have fond memories of having our life lit up by someone who saw our own unique gift. Yet I think how long it took me to recognize and *really* celebrate the strengths and gifts of my own daughter.

As parents of children with disabilities, we encounter many messages that discourage us from viewing our children as "gifted." For example, there is widespread agreement that, when we learn our child has a disability, we embark on a cycle of grief. The *high point* of this cycle is "acceptance." We know we have reached this pinnacle when we have learned to cope and be content with "small successes."

One of my parent friends in New Hampshire, tired of all this grief and coping, tells me she is working on developing a new cycle. I'm not sure what she has in mind, but I applaud the idea. How about a new cycle *beginning* with acceptance? What new possibilities might open up? Maybe there is a lesson for all of us in the way fleas are trained for the flea circus: Fleas are put into a jar with a lid. When they jump too high, they bump against the lid. After a while they learn to be careful and jump only so far.

Most of us have bumped up against the admonitions of others who caution us to be reasonable, not to expect too much, to accept our children's limitations. Rather than jump for joy in celebration of our children's accomplishments, we learn to contain our excitement. Inside a jar called the grief cycle, we aren't on the lookout for gifts. Tremendous victories become "small successes," and people learn not to jump too high. What would happen if the lid were removed and we knew we could jump in celebration without bumping against this artificial ceiling? If we jumped out of the jar altogether into a world where all people were already accepted for who they were—and for who they were not—might we begin to speak much more boldly about our children's gifts?

In a letter to the editor commenting on an article on tracking that had been featured in the *Boston Globe*, Dennis Geller wrote that the article mistakenly "assumes that giftedness is some attribute that applies to only a few students for whom it somehow is a uniform characteristic." He continues, "In the real world, few students are so monolithic" (*Boston Globe*, November 5, 1993).

Why is creating a new understanding of gifts and giftedness important? In exploring this question, *IntegrationNews*, a newsletter from the PEAK Parent Center in Colorado, quotes from "Don't All Children Have Gifts?" by David G. Myers, a research psychologist:

> Labels may be fables, but even fables can be self-fulfilling. . . . Let's drop these pernicious labels. Let's instead affirm all children's gifts. And let's get on with answering the question first posed by John Gardner in his book *Excellence*: "How can we provide opportunities and rewards for individuals of every degree of ability so that individuals at every level will realize their full potentialities, perform at their best, and harbor no resentment toward any other level?" By encouraging all children to believe in themselves—to define and develop their gifts—we keep faith with our democratic ideals while strengthening our creativity as a society.

Helping children define their gifts demands that we—their parents, teachers, and friends—develop a new way of speaking, beyond labels and prescriptions, that has the power to wake us up to each other's gifts. Judith Snow says, "Each of us has only one job—to become very, very good at speaking about our friends, about our relatives, and the people we love and know as being gifted people."

Janet Vohs is the parent of a child with special needs and the editor of NewsLine, *published by the Federation for Children with Special Needs. This article was originally printed in the December 1993 issue of* Newsline *and is reprinted with permission. Janet lives in Massachusetts.*

Different Road Child

by Susan Jordan

Your eyes are open wide
As you glide through your day
And you remember so much
Of what you see along the way

Your face lights up
at the beauty of a flower
As you embrace life with open arms
Ready to enjoy each precious hour

At times you come to me
With so much love inside
You glow

And smiling your radiant smile
Love spreads thickly in the air
In these special times we share
You temporarily dispel my cares

When you speak you use words
Other children still don't know
Your words reveal such brilliance
And your enthusiasm for learning always seems to grow

Then, all at once
When a rule is changed
Or a schedule bent
You lose control

You screech and scream
As though you were two
You fall apart just at the thought
Of something new

And often, when it's time to leave for school
We are late because you have misplaced
One important shoe
And you become frantic
As we search and search
And you are mad at yourself
Because you knew you knew
Just yesterday where you put the other shoe

You grasp science and math concepts brilliantly
Yet write b for d or q for p
Or leave out vowels entirely

You squirm and squirm
When you sit down to write
Turn your head this way and that
Your words run together without any space
And you write fast, as if in a race
And when you are done
Teachers comment "Slow down"
"Too sloppy" "Haste makes waste"
"You can do it if you just try"
But I know
Even though you're very bright
That that's all a lie
You do try, that's not why

So after only 2nd grade
You who are so bright
Have come to think
That you are dumb
Your hand won't write
What your mind commands
And the teacher's disapprovals
Don't help you understand

Until one day
I, as your parent
Finally realize
Your troubles won't just
Blow away
You are dyslexic
And must be treated that way
You must be shown
Different ways to learn
But it's nothing you can't do
Once we help you believe in you
And in time, you will be able
To read and write better too

Einstein had trouble in school
Leonardo and Rockefeller too
Yet they touched the world
And made it change
Perhaps because they saw
Things in a different way
They were able to free us
They made sense of what others
Couldn't see

They helped us grow
And so gained eternity

And you, my special child of eight
Who knows what you can give
If we encourage
Your special talents to live
Perhaps you'll invent the new wheel
If we can only help
You see and feel
How capable you really are
Then your dyslexia
Needn't hold you back
But can be conquered
And in time
You can compensate
For any lack
As adults learn to realize
The world isn't white and black

Susan Jordan is the mother of a child with dyslexia. This piece originally appeared in the 1989 issue of Their World *magazine and is reprinted with permission.*

Madison's First Day of School

by Joanne Crouse

I held my mom's hand, and together side by side

We walked to kindergarten with our heads held high.

You see, no one expected me to learn.

But here I am, and now it's my turn.

Mom and I sat down in those small little chairs,

The room got so quiet and people began to stare.

I guess it has to do with what mom and doc talked about.

He said, "Down syndrome" then the words faded out.

My mommy and I didn't let that bother us.

My sister and I get to ride the big bus.

I got a big kiss from Debbie, a neighbor of mine.

She came to my class to wish me "Good Luck."

The people once staring began to cheer up.

My mommy and me sat on the floor,

A couple times I ran through the door.

We colored and pasted with other moms and dads,

Sarah was alone and feeling real sad.

And when we all went out to play,

They learned more about me on that day.

Some watched me, others looked from the side,

And up I went that great big slide.

I didn't fall or cry in fear,

But down, down I came on my rear.

Some were amazed, I do suppose,

That I didn't land on my little nose.

But I can run and jump and see,

I can count and say my ABC's.

It's not as easy for me as you,

But I'm going to try to do it too.

Then we all went out to lunch.

I love kindergarten a Whole, Whole Bunch!!!!!

Joanne Crouse wrote this about her daughter's first day in a regular kinder-
garten class. She notes, "Acceptance is the key to success . . . and we accept
her and love her with no restrictions." Joanne lives in California.

My Brother

by Brian Netter

My brother, sometimes, is very cool. We share baseball cards and have a good collection. We both like video games and hate going to bed. My brother is 15 years old and was born on January 5, 1978. What's different about me and him is we look very different. Also we disagree a lot on things we should get. My brother has a learning disability that you can't tell anymore. I still think he is cool. My brother is nice.

Brian Netter wrote this about his older brother as part of a school assignment about his family and his life. He and his family live in California.

Battle Cries

by Nancy Eggleston

I'm sitting at my desk and I can hear the teacher say
That we'll be writing stories about dinosaurs today!
"Yes!" I cry, "that's great!" and I begin to sort my thoughts
While Teacher gives directions about subjects, form and plots.
But I'm already off in lands where dinosaurs roam free
And birds I can't identify soar past the highest tree.
"Due tomorrow, pictures, and at least two pages long. . . ."
I write it in my notebook, but somehow it will be wrong.
My dinosaur has scales, it is green and stands up tall. . . .
I climb inside my story, and put up my "daydream wall."
Together we fight battles, all mighty, fearless brave!
The two of us together, a kingdom we must save!
I sit upon his back and my magic sword is drawn
In a world where my classmates . . . suddenly are gone.
The ground begins to shake as we run t'ward the enemy line. . . .
Oh! My battle cries are horrid for a kid of only nine.
My teacher stands before me as I color on my page.
She wonders why she was asked to teach a child of my age.
That's when I look around to see the kids all watching me.
I wonder when they started working on geography?
Then in an upset voice she says, "You'll have to start again,
Your handwriting is terrible, and do it all in pen!"

It seems a hundred hours till the school bell rings at three.

I stuff my story in my bag, and mutter, "Yay, I'm free!"

I ride my bike home dreaming . . . about my dinosaur

And suddenly my watch says that it's twenty-five past four.

"I'm sorry, Mom," I say as I pour sand from in my shoe. . . .

"And I forgot my Math book!" Boy, Mom is looking blue.

Later in the evening when it's almost time for bed

Thoughts of Rex, my dinosaur, start filling up my head.

"Hey, Mom and Dad!" I holler, "Look at what I did today.

I wrote a story and colored it but I won't get an 'A.'"

My teacher says it's messy and I guess it's pretty dumb.

I fold it back in half and now I'm feeling rather glum.

My Dad says, "Hey, let's see it," and my Mom gives me a hug.

And soon she's typing while I color, sitting on the rug.

Rex, my dinosaur, takes life and runs a furious stride

In a little story in my heart that bursts with love and pride.

My parents gave encouragement, and then I heard them say,

"Perhaps, you'll be a writer or an artist, son, someday."

and

The ground begins to shake as we run t'ward the enemy line

Our battle cries are thunderous, my Mom and Dad's and mine.

Nancy Eggleston authored this after discovering that two of her children have attention deficit disorder. She says, "the discovery was a life saver for me because I'd always wondered why they both struggled so hard to pay attention and grasp everything in the classroom." She and her family live in California. A poem by her daughter Denise appears in chapter 4.

Our Special Son

by Joy Brown

When you are expecting a baby, you naturally assume, or at least hope, that when they are born, everything will be perfect. When our second son, Jamie, was born we never expected anything but that a—perfect baby. After all, our firstborn, Christopher, had been. He had even been an early talker, reading at the age of two.

When Jamie was born, he looked perfect. He weighed nine pounds, fourteen ounces and was a big healthy baby. We didn't even notice anything wrong with him until he started to get older. Physically, he developed fine. He even walked earlier than Chris did—he took his first steps at nine and a half months. Somewhere in my mind, though, something was telling me that something just wasn't quite right. Jamie wouldn't respond to his name when we would call it. I can't tell you the number of times that people would ask me if he could hear. I knew he could hear, because he would come running from another room for a favorite commercial or for his favorite Winnie the Pooh tape (which he still loves to this day).

Jamie didn't start talking like he should. He had very few words. I tried many times to tell the doctors that I felt something was wrong and I'd always hear the same thing: "Don't worry, he's young yet. He'll talk when he is ready." I knew in my heart that that just wasn't so. I knew something was wrong. I felt it all of the time.

About four months after his second birthday, I decided to have Jamie screened. . . . It was the most difficult call that I've ever had to make. . . . They tested various areas from cognitive abilities to his hearing. It turned out that my fears were well-founded. He was definitely lagging behind . . . in his speaking, cognitive, and communication abilities. His hearing and motor skills were fine. . . .

My husband and I had all of the classic reactions—blaming ourselves (but never each other), sadness, anger, grief, and hopelessness. The reaction from our families was so much more varied. The main thing that I have learned is that they cannot truly understand it all because they haven't gone through this themselves. My mother has always told me that she thinks the reason for Jamie's problems is emotional. She never gives that theory up. But if she would stop to think what we would have to have done to him, to traumatize him somehow so that he wouldn't talk, maybe then she wouldn't say that. Maybe that is her way of dealing with it.

I've had my sisters say, "If anyone can handle this, it would be you." (This, I think, is their way of saying, "I'm glad it happened to you and not to me.") There are many times when I don't feel like I can handle it and many times that I don't want to have to. Once, on a particularly bad day, I told my sister that I couldn't handle it anymore, not truly meaning it, just trying to explain the frustration I felt. She suggested that I put him in an institution. I could barely speak after that. I would NEVER consider that. I CAN handle this and I will. My biggest fear is that at some point in his life, he will have to live in some sort of institution. That, I know, is a normal fear for any family in our situation, but not one we like to talk about.

My wise family tells me, it could be worse. Yes, it could be. But it is my feeling that a lifetime struggle is certainly bad enough.

I look at this beautiful boy and I am angry. I've gotten over the "Why me?!" because this didn't happen to me—it happened to Jamie. I still sometimes wonder why him. Nothing he did caused this, yet, he has to deal with this, live with this his whole life. . . .

Jamie went to a special education preschool from the time

he was two and a half until this year when he was of kindergarten age and entered grade school. Sending him to school at
such a young age was a difficult thing for me to do. . . . I drove
him to school for a while because I didn't think that he could
handle riding the bus. . . . He would cry when I left. I just
wanted to grab him and take him home with me. After a short
while, he was riding the bus and loving it. The first day that
the bus drove away with him, I just sat down and cried and
cried. He, to this day, adores riding the bus. And it can still
bother me if I watch his bus pull away with him. Sometimes,
little things like that can still trigger something. My child is
not normal and he may never be. No one knows what the
future holds for him.

I have learned many, many things since having Jamie. First
of all, ALWAYS trust yourself! You are the one who knows your
child best. You are the professional when it comes to them. Do
not be intimidated by the "professionals" or believe that their
word is the final one, just because they have the job or the
degree. Learn to question, to speak up, to be an advocate for
your child, for no one cares for your child as you do yourself.
One thing that I have learned is to become involved. I looked
for a support group for parents in my situation and to my
amazement there wasn't one. So I helped start one. To be able
to talk to someone who truly understands is invaluable. . . .

I find myself wondering what Jamie would be like if he
were "normal." What would he be like without the tantrums,
the behavior problems, the constant teaching, trips to the
speech therapist, with words?! What kind of child would he be
like? I don't know. What I do know is what kind of a child that
he is. He is a very beautiful, affectionate, loving, and intelli-
gent boy. He can spell, write, count, name his colors, say his
alphabet and he gains new words all of the time. Not long ago,
he had only twenty-five words and many more frustrations
and tantrums. There were days of dumped coffee cans, "art

work" on the kitchen walls and cupboards, dumped milk, broken glasses and sleep problems. He would sometimes get up in the middle of the night and stay up for hours. He has finally been sleeping through the night for several months now. A big milestone for us. He still has some behavior problems and there is always something new to tackle, but as he grows and matures, he does seem to do just that! Grow and mature. At age four, he even called me mom for the very first time! There was a time I didn't even know if he would ever be able to say that. So, you see, something that one day felt like the end of the world, you laugh at the next.

Dealing with a child with special needs was something I never expected to happen in my life. But it did. And we deal with it the best we can. The grief still comes at times. I find that it all goes in cycles. There is much sadness, yet much happiness. There is much frustration when people look at Jamie and see a normal child and then he'll do something they don't quite expect and they will give him and me a strange look. How can they understand? It hurts. It makes me angry.

By night, I am so tired because having a child like Jamie is emotionally draining. . . . But Jamie has progressed so far in the last year or two and is doing so much that I am again hopeful. Hope—it is a very powerful coping device. There is nothing like the look in his eyes or the look on his face when he is praised for a good job, or you understand something that he is trying to tell you.

If I had had a choice, I would not have a child with "special needs." I would have a normal family that could go anywhere or spend a Christmas with our relatives that was peaceful and free of tension. People have said time and again that these children are special blessings for special parents. I believe that these are people who have "normal" kids who are trying to make it better for us that don't. I am not any more special than you and I do not find that this is a special blessing. . . . I would trade it all in a second if my child could be "normal" and live his life as such! I love Jamie more than anything in the world. And I will always do everything in my power to help him get better to have that chance at a normal life!

Joy Brown finished writing this essay when Jamie was 6 years old. She comments, "My hope with writing it was to someday share it with others so that they could understand what we went through and our feelings." She and her family live in Iowa.

The Kid's A Hero
by Gail Harrison

A frequent flyer

Through the Wall of Fear.

Though a native of Non-Conformity,

Bravely he faces

The everyday event

Of being different.

An Original

From Originality,

Ingeniously covering

The confusion

of incomprehension.

Creatively disguising

Pain as defiance,

Bewilderment as comedy.

Artistically cultivating

Sensitivity and awareness,

Compulsory by common

occurrence

A survivor with

Endearing endurance,

Beloved by those,

Who finally recognized him

As a stranger,

In a foreign land,

And decided to

Teach him the language.

Gail Harrison is the parent of a child with a learning disability. This poem was originally published in the 1992 issue of Their World *and is reprinted with permission.*

Untitled

by Paula Barnett

My son was diagnosed 6 years ago with a learning disability. The hardest part has not been the hours spent helping with homework, etc. It has been the tremendous amount of patience that is involved. The hardest part of all has been dealing with the teachers. Each year I have had to start all over and educate the teachers as to his special needs and requirements for learning. I feel as though they think I am an overprotective mother trying to make things easy for her son. I sincerely hope that soon in his school life a teacher will take a special interest in a special boy. So far the best example of sincere caring about him and whether he succeeds other than his family has been his school bus driver. One day a teacher told me that I would be "LUCKY" if my son graduated from high school and to be glad for that. Well, together we'll show her!

Paula Barnett wrote this out of her frustration with her son's education. He has learning disabilities that interfere with his processing of information. Paula and her son live in Tennessee.

Karl

by Sandra Urso

My name is Karl, I am five
Sometimes, I get scared, I need to hide,
Away from adults, who can't be trusted
they might hurt me, I can't let them.
I can't sit still, easily distracted
They call me hyperactive.

Sometimes mommy gets very mad.
I wonder, am I bad?
I try to be good, if being still is good.
I try, try I know I should.
Teachers don't like me, I feel stupid.
I can't seem to wait, do what they say,
Will I fail again, another day?
They put me in time out,
They say I need to listen.
I would, if I could But
my mind, body is racing.
I feel angry, hurt, confused,
Kinds don't like me, I can't stick to the rules.

My stomach all tied up in knots,

How can I be all that I'm not?

The noise, compounds the frustration.

I cry, I run, everything's out of control.

I want my mommy!

I want to go home!

I need to feel safe, someone tell me it's going to be ok.

My head hurts real bad.

Give me a hug,

A friend to play.

Mommy, do you love me?

Again,

    Tomorrow's

        Another Day.

Sandra Urso, Karl's mother, composed this to describe Karl. He has attention deficit hyperactivity disorder, has difficulty with gross and fine motor skills, and is emotionally immature. They live in Connecticut.

Off the Top of My Head

by Jane Corn

There are several issues that often cause major problems and adjustments after a child is found to have a learning disability. From a parent's perspective, there is often a mourning period as the parent comes to terms with the fact that his or her child is less than his idealized vision or seems to have serious limitations. There is also often a great deal of guilt and questions about what caused the disability. I know in my case that I went back over every event from birth on and wondered if a particular event caused any neurological injury that could explain my son's attention deficit disorder. Talking to specialists and reading through research materials and books helped to alleviate my fears somewhat, but not entirely. At some point, I found that I simply had to stop worrying, accept the reality and move on from there. Only then, was I able to see that my grief and guilt were far more extreme than they needed to be and that the reality of attention deficit disorder, at least in our case, was not so terrible. Although we had to work at finding ways to help him compensate for his reduced attention span, our son is a bright, creative child who is learning and achieving on the same level as his peers.

From the child's perspective, there can be problems living with a label and struggling with self-esteem issues connected to being "different." I think it is a great advantage if a child can see that attention deficit disorder is not just a negative but can have many positive attributes as well. While our son has more difficulty paying attention to individual tasks for long periods of time, he often notices unique details about situations or the environment that we would never notice because of his constantly changing attention. He is also very creative and imaginative (there is some research indicating that creativity may be associated with attention deficit disorder). He is alert, active and excited about all the possibilities in the world. These traits probably contributed to his receiving an enthusiasm award in scouting (which excited him far less than the huge water gun he also received that has become the envy of his scout mates).

We found it useful to limit the number of people who knew our son had attention deficit disorder. In many instances this would not be possible, but many children can fit in if they are diagnosed early, shown ways to compensate for their disability and given medication as needed. We did tell teachers, school administrators, etc., but limited the number of parents and peers who know. It was not necessary and we felt that it reduced the chances of our son being labeled.

The next most important thing a parent can do is to help his or her child find a talent, interest or skill that can be developed. It can take quite a bit of time and searching to find just the right activity and what may work one year may not be a good fit the next. Our son has participated in gymnastics, art classes, baseball, scouting and soccer. He has remained interested in baseball and art. We also read to him from his earliest years and found this an excellent way to develop attention skills. It is best if the activity can be somewhat open-ended (art is a good example) and taught in a nonjudgmental atmosphere. Our son's first art experience was a class called Drawing with Imagination where the students were rewarded for drawing the wildest, least realistic pictures they could. Since our son had a great deal of insecurity about making pictures that looked "right," it was a relief to be in a class where this was not a priority.

Of course, it also makes a great deal of difference if the child knows he is more than just "a learning disability." So we use the label "attention deficit disorder" only when we have to. The rest of the time we talk about specific areas to work on like spending more time completing a task, paying attention for longer periods of time, etc. This seems to work best.

We also search out role models who have achieved in spite of similar disabilities. We have learned that Einstein, John Kennedy and many other famous figures have or may have had attention deficit disorder. We found a tape, "Young Mr. Edison" (starring Mickey Rooney), that was a valuable resource. We watched and discussed the movie with our son. In spite of all sorts of problems because of his tendency to get into trouble due to his inquisitiveness and impulsiveness, Edison is portrayed as someone who eventually succeeded.

We have gotten reactions from teachers who feel that attention deficit disorder is merely a convenient "label" to explain away a child's laziness or unwillingness to pay attention rather than a real condition. While this is not true, we have done our best to provide teachers with materials containing tested learning strategies, coping techniques, etc. to help children with ADD succeed in school. It is never a matter of giving these children an "edge" over the other students, but rather a chance to be on an equal level. In many cases, this means making a simple change like seating the child with ADD at the front of the classroom where distractions are minimal. In other instances, it may mean letting the child tape-record a story rather than writing it (assuming, of course, that he will continue to work on his penmanship skills) until his writing ability catches up. It makes a great deal of difference if a teacher is understanding, compassionate and encouraging to children with ADD.

Jane Corn wrote this to help other parents benefit from her experience with the issues surrounding her son's attention deficit disorder. She and her family live in Indiana.

Bouncing Ball

by *Joanne Harris*

She's bouncing off walls, Superball gone insane,
She runs through your world like an off rail freight train,
Interruptions are constant, tantrums galore,
When it's time to do homework, she's gone, out the door.

The drama is constant, oh her foot fell asleep,
She moans and she wails, the theatrics run deep,
School is a nightmare, the teachers are lost,
If they only could see, she is worth the cost.

She is brighter than most, as most of them are
And with patience and love, I know she'll go far.
But the crap I must take from "WELL MEANING FRIENDS"
"Don't let her do that," Oh, **these rules that she bends.**

"YOU'RE NOT A GOOD PARENT," "Your child's really rude,"
"Her temper's outrageous," "Her hand's in her food."
She hears this and wonders, just what's wrong with me?
I tell her "You're special," you have ADHD.

"Now ADHD is a gift from above.
It teaches us grown-ups how to strengthen our LOVE.

It helps teach your teachers no two kids are the same,
You have awesome energy, that could bring you great fame."

You don't need much sleep, you never wear down.
You're silly and funny, when you act like a clown.
You've felt lots of pain from what people have said,
But you pray for those people when you go to bed.

So you try every day to make a fresh start,
For God gifted you with an extra big heart,
As I look at my child, she sees through my soul,
My heart feels like bursting, as I realize my goal.

I know this young girl like no one else could,
She's a blessing to me, she's strong and she's good.
So I'll love her and guide her through the worst of the worst,
And she'll make a great woman (if I don't kill her first).

I'm kidding of course, 'cause I know what's to be,
When I look in her eyes, I see a reflection of Me.

---

*Joanne Harris wrote this to her daughter, Heather Hauri, who has been diag-
nosed with attention deficit hyperactivity disorder. She wrote this poem for
Heather to remind her daughter "that she is not a material thing that can
be replaced for happiness but she is a 'Special Child' and I love her." A poem
by Heather appears in chapter 1. They live in California.*

A New Beginning

by Jocelyn Steele

A new beginning is something different in every one of us. It's the time when something special happens in your life that might change it.

My new beginning was when I learned that my sister was handicapped. I realized why she would do things at a slower pace, although with determination and with my help and that of my parents, I share with her many new, exciting beginnings.

There are people in our world who don't understand what it's like to have a handicapped sister or brother, or to experience feelings I have at times, such as sadness, hurt, frustration, and happiness. My sister's humor, loving care, and kindness make up for her disability. Her humor displays itself through her actions and words. Life's simple pleasures can bring out happiness in her and those around her. My sister is special. She has taught me things that really matter, things like love, patience, kindness, generosity, forgiveness, and values. She will always be my best friend.

Each day can be a special day if you want to make it so. I have learned that through my sister's accomplishments. She takes each day in her own special stride. She accomplishes goals that are set for her. It may only take a day for me to read a book; it may take her a week or more. It took me at the age of five about a week to learn how to ride a bicycle; she is still trying at the age of nine.

Life with my sister has opened my eyes to the world around me and to appreciate her and what life is about. If everyone would stop and smell the roses, and be considerate of other people's feelings, it would be a much better world to live in.

My sister has Down syndrome. If my sister could describe herself, I believe she would say this:

There's something different about me that makes me different, at least on the outside. I have an extra chromosome in every cell of my body. The extra chromosome changes my appearance a little. My eyes are slightly slanted, my little finger turns inward, my speech is delayed, and sometimes I get frustrated when people don't listen to understand me. I have low muscle tone that sometimes causes me to be clumsy. I am able to accomplish everything I set my mind and heart to do. I'm not just a fluke of nature like the doctors told my parents when I was born. I wish people could really see the true me. It would make it easier for parents with other people like me not to feel sad or guilty or ashamed. I love my parents and my sister. They make me feel like I'm no different than anyone else.

Every day can be a new beginning if you make it happen.

Jocelyn Steele entered this essay in a school PTA contest when she was in 8th grade. She won second place. She lives in California.

My Daughter

by Dianne Whitman

I'd like you to meet my daughter. Her name is Robin. Robin is very kind and sweet. She is polite and has good judgment about people and situations. She is very mature and wise. She is honest, very pretty and popular. She is well liked by her peers and adults. Robin likes to talk to her friends on the phone a lot (we had to get call-waiting) and she likes to go places and do things with her friends. If you were to meet Robin you would think she was like any other 12-year-old kid. Only Robin has a learning disability.

She can read very little. She forgets a lot of things since her memory is poor. Robin spells most words the way they sound (like SORRY would be SRE), and she has trouble with math.

This makes school very hard for her. She is in a regular classroom and goes to the resource room for help in math, spelling and reading. She has, however, been in a special day class in 2nd, 3rd & 4th grades, but she developed such poor self-esteem and depression that I finally put her back in her home school in a regular class with Resource Specialists Program (RSP) help. She came alive again.

Even though many things have to be modified for her in the regular classroom (oral tests, less homework, someone to help her take notes and help her with writing reports, etc.) it is where she belongs. I only wish I had realized it sooner.

You see, Robin knows the other kids can read better and do math she cannot do, and they can spell better, but she has learned that this does not make a better person. At recess, lunch and after school when she and her friends do things together and go places, she is just like the other kids.

In fact, sometimes I think she is wiser and more mature.

I think at times her learning disability bothers me more than her. I sometimes feel so sad for her when I see her struggle to read or see a letter she has written where almost every word is spelled wrong. I wish so much that she didn't have to struggle, but I know she probably always will.

I try to learn as much as I can about learning disabilities so I can help her and educate parents with "normal" kids, because most really have no idea what the child or the parent endures every day. I've come across more than one parent who will make a comment that really hurts, like "You should know your phone number by now," "Can't you read that?" They just have no idea how hard these kids try.

But Robin doesn't seem to let any of this get her down. She is always willing to try and she applies herself and tries to learn as much as she can.

She does not seem embarrassed by her learning disability. She has learned to get by rather well. She will have her friends write letters for her so they are spelled right. She also asks them for help in class, to take notes, etc.

She lets her friends know she has a learning disability and it's nothing to be ashamed of because Robin knows she is very kind and sweet. She is polite and has good judgment about people and situations. She is honest, very pretty and popular. She is liked by her peers and adults. Robin is like any other 12-year-old kid and when she is an adult it won't matter what kind of student she was. What will matter is what kind of person she is.

Dianne Whitman wrote this when her daughter, Robin, was in the seventh grade. She wrote it to show how proud she is "of the kind of person she has become despite the many obstacles she has had to endure." They live in California.

Where Have All the Fathers Gone

by Paul Becker

"To be or not to be
That is the question
Whether tis nobler to" hide your head
in the sand or face the problem head on
This I pose to fathers of dyslexic children

Ever since my daughter was diagnosed, some nine years ago, I have been seeking the answer to a puzzle. Wherefore art the fathers? or Where have all the fathers gone?

In attendance at conferences and meetings sponsored by the New York Branch of the Orton Dyslexia Society I see only the female parent. The father is always "too busy." Please do not take these statements as a condemnation of all fathers, but I get the feeling that the majority of fathers are either ashamed of their handicapped child or feel guilty that they in some way contributed to the problem. Well, dad, face facts. You had a hand in bringing this child into this world. Don't shuck your responsibilities now.

Go with your wife to parent-teacher conferences. If you feel uncomfortable speaking, say nothing. Your mere attendance is enough.

Read with your child. You take a paragraph and let your son or daughter do the same. Encourage, do not discourage. If you yourself have a problem reading don't be ashamed to explain that to your child.

Learn more about dyslexia. By educating yourself you will be able to help your child understand his or her problem. Go to parent meetings and conferences to find out what other parents are doing and feeling.

Please, just don't sit back and do nothing. Your lack of action gives the appearance of not caring.

TO BE OR NOT TO BE
ONLY YOU CAN ANSWER THE QUESTION.

Paul Becker wrote this article for the Winter 1994 edition of Dyslexia, *the newsletter of the New York Branch of the Orton Dyslexia Society. He is first vice-president of the society and often expresses his frustration over the lack of attendance by fathers at team meetings and group meetings.*

Chapter 6

Teachers' Voices

This final chapter turns the spotlight on those who teach students with disabilities. Teachers, who are at times criticized for lack of sensitivity and patience and at other times praised as the "one who made a difference," deserve to be heard. Like any other profession, there are good teachers, great teachers, and poor teachers. As one contributor, Estelle Epstein, puts it, the best teachers "are constantly trying to find better ways to reach children with learning problems." They are characterized by their students as having patience, perseverance, creativity, and the ability to recognize and focus on the strengths as well as the problems of the children with whom they work.

The voices offer a view of teachers seldom seen by parents or their students.

Come Follow Me

by Ellen L. Humbert

I met a child who could not see.
"Come," she called, "come follow me!"
She turned . . . she smiled . . . she touched my hand.
She seemed to know I'd understand.

"Child," I said, "where shall we go?
What are these things you seek to know?
And tell me . . . if this be the day
who is there to lead the way?"

"Come," she called, "come and see!
Hurry . . . come and follow me!"

She laughed . . . she danced . . . she sang her song.
I followed after her all day long,
and we told stories . . . we shared dreams . . .
We traveled many miles it seems.

And sometimes, in her need to know
she'd rush ahead, to touch-and-go . . .
trusting me . . . believing all . . .
I waited there . . . I heard her call.

"Come . . . follow . . . come and see!
Hurr. . . . come and follow me!"

Do you suppose we all might be
like this child who could not see . . .
reaching out to take the hand
of someone who would understand?

And could we walk, no matter where . . .
believing in the promise there?
Could we love, and trust, and be
children calling "Follow me . . . ?"

"Come," she called, "come and see!
Hurry . . . come and follow me!"

Oh child . . . I watched you through the years.
I saw your triumphs and your tears.
I treasured every day with you . . .
but tell me . . . who was leading who?

For you . . . a child who could not see
looked into the heart of me.
Oh, for sight . . . that I could know
how to help another grow.

"Come," she called, "come and see!
Hurry . . . come and follow me!"

Ellen L. Humbert lives in Arizona and is a teacher of students with disabilities. This poem is about a little girl whom she taught for many years. It was originally published in Teaching Exceptional Children, *Summer 1991, and is reprinted here with the permission of the Council for Exceptional Children.*

Untitled

by Dana Blackhurst

Teaching in this field over the last eleven years has been quite remarkable now that I take the time to reflect back. I have never really taken time before to think about what I do here with these children. I look forward to and enjoy every day. I find my position interesting because it allows me to be myself. Although I cannot explain all of these things I do as a teacher, or even as a person, with the children, I do know that I always enjoy seeing them in class. It is never I or me, but we as a team.

The classroom is comparable to an amusement park to me, each day like a roller coaster with many ups and downs. I smile when I think of the things we have done together and the accomplishments of the children. To me, the children I teach are the neatest and most interesting people in the world. They are among the most sensitive and compassionate human beings you will ever meet. I wish all people could see the work through their eyes and experience how they solve problems.

Through my years of teaching, I have learned that I do not "accommodate." I stress tenacity, self-discipline, and "going the extra mile." Each student is dealt certain cards in life and must learn to do what it takes to play that hand. They must disregard the classification of "disabled" realizing they have gifts and talents to offer their community and the world. During their education they will challenge teachers and professors to think differently about teaching methods and then to put these methods to work.

These are also the students who have what today's work force needs—high energy. I believe in the phrase, "Hire the hyperactive, you will get more work out of him." Sure they will make mistakes, but does this make them any different from the other employees? What they will contribute to the business community far outweighs any possible mistakes.

As I sit in my classroom and observe these children, I am amazed to think that I may be the catalyst that stimulates the thought of the next Carl Sagan. Every day from a classroom in Greenville, South Carolina, I can take the students to Zimbabwe, Africa, an NHL hockey game or any points in between, simply through conversation. I believe in dreams and daydreaming and my life is richer by the dreams my students share with me.

I demand much from our students including that they learn to demand of themselves. I do not believe they are different from other children in their dreams and desires. I do, however, see them as the uncommon thinkers. The thinkers who are fun to be around, who are independent in their thoughts and actions and who do not always follow the pack. These thinkers dare to stand out, to try, to fail, and to pick themselves up again. They dare to live life to the fullest. This is the gift these children have to offer. As I work with each child, helping to build self-esteem, and teaching them the art of learning, I wait for the "breakthrough" moment; that moment when they realize they can do anything. At that point it is wonderful to sit back and watch them take off. These are the times I fantasize that each child is a thoroughbred racehorse simply needing a lot of guidance and a little coaxing to help them out in front and take the lead.

It is difficult to explain what I have done over the years, teaching at Kildonan School, Sandhills Academy, the Jemicy School, and now at Camperdown Academy. Maybe I cannot explain it—I just do it. I come to the amusement park each day, filled with anticipation of the new attractions awaiting me.

Dana Blackhurst is headmaster of the Camperdown Academy in South Carolina.

Special Ed

by William D. Hoskin

Ryan waved his paper,
excited
to show me his story about

two mrean bilogast
where studing
hunpback whale..
A lod noise like a siren,
a lod sreak
and it was silent.
A big clod of blood
ment a shark frenzy.

Oh, yeah! And then, Ryan?

We look don a grat white
cumming up for a nuter hit.
He tied the sper to a rope
I felt the roop titen and
I wes getting pulld.
The sark stared to slo don.
I manged to cut free.

Wow, Ryan!

William Hoskin is one of the founders and a board member of the Norman Howard School for Children with Dyslexia in Rochester, New York. He wrote this about one of the students at the school to contribute to an increasing understanding of those who struggle with the annoyance and frustration of a learning disability.

All in a Year's Work

by Maxine Powell

Myriads of looks
On upturned faces,
Hundred of things lost
A thousand places.

Hold my hand?
Turn me loose!
Which way to the
Red caboose?

Show me I can. . .
Then make me do it!
Laugh with me,
When I get through it.

Empty halls and
Quiet spaces,
Hopes taken wing
To far-flung places.

Maxine Powell is a teacher of social studies and language development at Camperdown Academy. She lives in South Carolina.

Tiger's Eye

by Nadine Sabra Meyer

Now that it's Spring, I think of Jordan, his fists blooming
an offering, torn daffodils browned already at the stem's
mouth. I put these broken-necked tokens in a serious fluted
vase, carefully balancing the heads and Jordan announces like
a ritual, "No homework! Right?" and we start into motion. I
circle behind him and straighten his shoulders, adjust his
paper, insist on his numerals, and he drops his pencil, man-
ages out of his chair, and when I'm back, he's started his paper
on the wrong side.

Sometimes
it was dandelions. When he'd finished off some poor neighbor's annuals, or maybe just when it turned Summer, he
started in with the dandelions, the vase sprouting tight yel-
low-petal tiers grown limp in his fists and the balls of loose
seed-fluff. The sun's direct rays heated our classroom like a
greenhouse, Jordan's hand going like a bee in his shirt, to
announce connections between fractions and decimals, area
and perfect squares, dividing and calculators or just dividing
and doing it in your head, anything to not write it down, his
brilliance drawing circles and knots in the air around our
heads. And on paper his brilliance came out tangled in knots
of long division half done wrong in his head. I straightened
his back, kicked his feet under his desk, pressed his numbers
into columns that squirmed and got mad, none of the multiplication facts staying in his head but changing and rising like
steam out of reach and Jordan exploded. But he came back
during recess and we started again, got out hundreds, tens
and ones and shared the "Powers of Ten" with imaginary
people on index cards, recording blocks of paper 'til it made

sense again and he could do it and showed off, the impatient color of Summer in his face.

Now that it's Spring, I think again of Jordan's offerings, the dandelions, dry from a weekend without water, I threw out the back door, stiff stems and loose heads, tiger's eye yellow and brown. I think of those who confuse flowers and weeds, and I think of those of us who blur, with bright yellow blooms (that never come in straight lines), the difference, and who, with balls of seed, with the right touch, with the touch of the wind, rise sending thousands of tiny points that spread through Summer.

Nadine Sabra Meyer, who is herself dyslexic, graduated from the Johns Hopkins Writing Seminars Department. She composed the above essay about a student she taught at the Jemicy School. She lives in Maryland.

Empowering

by Virginia Meador

"Mrs. Meador, what is 7 x 8?" Eric asks.
   "You tell me the answer and I'll
   tell you if you are right."
Eric learns he has the answers within himself.

"Mrs. Meador, what does it matter that snowflakes have six
sides?" Paul says with eighth grade boredom.
   "This snowy day has real magic floating from the sky.
   Come and see hexagonal uniqueness."
Paul may begin to see beauty hidden in plain sight.

"Mrs. Meador, bugs are so YUCKY and you want ME to pin
one in the box!" Mollie says in disgust.
   "Go ahead, pin him down even if you have to use a
   plastic glove to hold him."
Mollie learns of her own growing courage.

"Mrs. Meador, it's not fair that I'm dyslexic," cried Andrea in
despair.
   "I too am dyslexic; look and see how I have made it a
   strength."
Andrea may come to appreciate her own specialness.

"Mrs. Meador, your dyslexia is so evident," Harris says as I
read a 9 for a 6.

"My mistakes show that I have traveled the same road

as you travel. Watch me work with my imperfections."
Harris sees that he may be able. . . .

*Virginia Meador is a science teacher at Camperdown Academy in South
Carolina.*

To See What You See

by Estelle Pottern Epstein

I see you, child. I hear you.

I know the road you travel.

Baby steps, not giant steps

        carry you along.

I'll be there, child. Yes, near you.

Together we'll unravel each concept

        piece by piece

      until all parts belong.

I know how hard you work, child.

Concepts harder than they seem.

I'll cheer you on day by day,

        enhance your self-esteem.

I try to see what you see, child.

How can I simplify?

So one day I may hear you say,

        "That's as easy as pie!"

You shall set the pace, child.

I'll pick you up if you should fall.

Mentor, guide and friend to you,

              I hear your voiceless call.

Like the tortoise and the hare,

              the race is clearly won

when the runner reaches the goal,

              not when the race has begun.

Estelle Pottern Epstein has taught for more than 25 years in regular first-grade and third-grade classrooms and has worked as a teaching supervisor at Salem State College in Massachusetts. She feels that "dedication, understanding, and inspirational skill is the key" in working with children with special needs.

List of Contributors

Grateful acknowledgment is made to the following individuals and associations for permission to reprint unpublished and copyrighted material:

– Jesse W. Adcox for "Where Does the Time Go?" and "The Twig"

– Rosalie Marie Bolenbaugh Baker for "Small Blessings"

– Paula Barnett for "Untitled"

– Belva Barnhardt for "What Is a Learning Disability?"

– Beach Center on Families and Disabilities for Parent-to-Parent Program List (see appendix D)

– Jenifer Becker for "Misunderstood Child"

– Paul Becker for "Where Have All the Fathers Gone"

– Chris Biner for "My Essay"

– Margaret Birch for "High School Graduation"

– Dana Blackhurst for "Untitled"

– Julie Blanchard for "Dyslexia"

– Maryann Blust for "How I See ADD"

– Noreen Boyle for "Voices Through the Bedroom Walls"

– Richard Brodeur for "Why"

– Dale Brown for "Harness" and "Learning to Dance"

– Joy Brown for "Our Special Son"

– Tara Cashin for "Last"

– Nancy Edwards Clay for "Left Brain/Right Brain, Half Insane" and "The Little Glass Girl"

– Jane Corn for "Off the Top of My Head"

– Council for Exceptional Children for "Some Thoughts on Learning Disabilities" (author unknown) and "Come Follow Me" by Ellen L. Humbert

– Joanne Crouse for "Madison's First Day of School"

– Julie Daniels for "Key to Life"

– Mary Daum for "Bedtime Wishes" and "The List"

– Timothy DeMars for "Untitled"

– Richard Devine for "Teacher, Teacher"

– Denise Eggleston for "Mandy Michelle Misty Moore"

– Nancy Eggleston for "Battle Cries"

– Amy Epstein for "Untitled"

– Estelle Pottern Epstein for "To See What You See"

– Carvell Estriplet for "The Sobbing Cry"

– Federation for Children with Special Needs for "Help for Parents" by Susan Lunden and "Bundles of Gifts" by Janet Vohs

– Joseph Federico for "I Get Steamed"

– Ellen Federman for "Life with Learning Disabilities"

– Chris Ferrino for "The Autism Book"

– Michael Fleischer for "A Letter from a Learning Disabled Child"

– Louise Fundenberg for "Nothing Succeeds Like Success"

– Lindsay Gaines for "Untitled"

– Catharine Grace for "Untitled" and "The Fear Within Me—A Real Life Horror Story"

– Brenda Harris for "Letting Go"

– Joanne Harris for "Bouncing Ball"

– Kimberly Harter-Key for "Speaking Up" and "I Am Somebody"

– Heather Hauri for "Mommy"

– Chris Hines for "Sidewalk; Riffs Begin on Words"

– Darren Hines for "Untitled"

– Kathleen Holmes for "Living with a Learning Disability"

– William D. Hoskin for "Special Ed"

– Eli Jackson for "I Can"

– Emily Perl Kingsley for "Welcome to Holland"

– Thomas Konczal for "ADDvantages of ADD?"

– Kristina Kops for "My Book Says God"

– Gavriel Kullman for "The Great Dolphin"

– Robert A. Lane, Jr., for "An Abstract Apology"

– Learning Disabilities Association of America for "Driving Ambition" by Jim H. Shreve and "How Our Parents Have Helped Us: Positive and Negative" by Gale L. Bell

– Thomas Lennon for "My Learning Disability"

– Jessica Lenz for "Follow the Road" and "We the People"

– Joan A. Levine for "LD"

- Kay Lipper for "Proudest Moments"

- Scott M. Martin for "It's Not an Excuse!" and "On the Hill with Spirits"

- Virginia Meador for "Empowering"

- Lynne McCarthy for "So What!"

- Caitlin McCormick for "Testing Day at Jemicy"

- Anson McNulty for "What You Need to Have to Be Dyslexic"

- Nadine Sabra Meyer for "Tiger's Eye"

- Matthew Mills for "Out with the D a m Frustration"

- National Center for Learning Disabilities, Inc., for "Exploring New Beginnings," by Elizabeth Lord; "Me," by Emily Gross; "There is More to Life Than a Learning Disability," by Karen Klein; "From a Mother to her Son," by Laura Bulger; "Someone Please Hear My Cry," by Jean Carlson; "Different Road Child," by Susan Jordan; "Imprisoned Bug," by Sheri Miller; "The Fable of the Dragon Dyslexia," by Richard Bogia; "Untitled," by Larry Volk; "A Seagull," by Karen Chrzescyanek; "The Gifted LD Child," author unknown; "Some Teachers Really Did Make a Difference," by Chris Reilly; and "The Kid's A Hero" by Gail Harrison

- Brian Netter for "My Brother"

- Avi Ostchega for "Days" and "One Word"

- Matthew Payne for "From Behind Closed Doors"

- Maxine Powell for "All in a Year's Work"

- Jeffrey Proctor for "COURAGE: Fighting My Fears"

- Phillip Russell for "Books! Books! Books!"

- Andrea Rose Schneider for "Being Without and Losing Out" and "I Am a Rock"

– Michael Sapienza for "WORK"

– Heather Susan Schwam for "No One Can Tell"

– Kate Shannon for "Discovering Paths" and "Melodic Logic"

– Amy Smith for "Untitled"

– Jeremy Smith for "Speech Given to the School Board"

– Nick Stead for "Untitled"

– Jocelyn Steele for "A New Beginning"

– Threshold Program, Lesley College for "Friendship" and "Life"

– Mike Uhrich for "What's on the Inside"

– Elizabeth Upsher for "Untitled"

– Sandra Urso for "Karl"

– F. Shea Weber for "Untitled"

– Liz Welker for "If I'm Smart, Why do I FEEL so STUPID?"

– Dianne Whitman for "My Daughter"

– Robert Wilson for "ADD: What's It Like?"

– Virginia Wise for "Dyslexia"

SPECIAL THANKS

W e wish to thank the following associations, schools, and newsletters for their participation. Many people went out of their way not only to encourage individuals to submit their writings, but also to acknowledge the efforts of students and family members. Contact names, addresses, and statements of purpose are included (if available) for information purposes only.

ADD-ONS
P.O. Box 675
Frankfort, IL 60423
815-469-8567
Mary Daum, President
     A newsletter dedicated to providing education and support to those living with attention deficit disorder (ADD).

ATTENTION, Please!
Route 1, Box 1913
Lopez Island, WA 98261
     A newsletter for children with ADD.

Beach Center on Families and Disabilities
The Family Connection
University of Kansas
3111 Haworth Hall
Lawrence, KS 66045
1-800-854-4938
 A referral agency for families with members who have cognitive and behavioral challenges.

Boston University
LD Support Services
19 Deerfield Street
Boston, MA 02115
Richard Goldhammer, Coordinator

Camperdown Academy
501 Howell Road
Greenville, SC 29615
803-244-8899
Dana Blackhurst, Headmaster
 A school for children with average to above-average IQs who have different learning styles.

The Carroll School
P.O. Box 280
Baker Bridge Road
Lincoln, MA 01773
617-259-8342
Thomas Needham, Headmaster
 An independent day school for children ages 6–19 who are primarily language disabled and/or dyslexic.

Children with Attention Deficit Disorders (CHADD)
499 NW 70th Avenue
Suite 308
Plantation, FL 33317

Council for Exceptional Children (CEC)
1920 Association Drive
Reston, VA 22091-1589

The Crossroads School
1681 North Valley Road
P.O. Box 730
Paoli, PA 19301
215-296-6765
Dottie Mazullo, Supervisor of Special Programs
    A small, private, nonprofit coeducational school for young-
sters ages 5–15 whose intelligence falls within the average to
superior range. These children learn differently and have difficulty
in conventional schools.

Developmental Resource Center
2741 Van Buren Street
Hollywood, FL 33020
Dr. Deborah Levy, Director

Federation for Children with Special Needs
95 Berkeley Street
Suite 104
Boston, MA 02116

Parents of Gifted/LD Children
2420 Eccleston Street
Silver Spring, MD 20902
    A nonprofit parent support group.

The Jemicy School
11 Celadon Road
Owings Mills, MD 21117
410-653-2700
Steve Wilkins, Headmaster

The Kildonan School
Box 294
Amenia, NY 12501
914-373-8111
Ronald A. Wilson, Headmaster
A coeducational boarding and day school for students with
learning differences arising from dyslexia.

Learning Disabilities Association of America (LDA)
4156 Library Road
Pittsburgh, PA 15234
A national organization devoted to defining and finding
solutions for the broad spectrum of learning problems.

Learning Disabilities Association of Massachusetts
1275 Main Street
Waltham, MA 02154
Teresa Citro, Executive Director

Learning Disabilities Association of Washington
17530 NE Union Hill
Suite 100
Redmond, WA 98052

The Oakland School
Boyd Tavern
Keswick, VA 22947
804-293-9059
A coeducational, success-oriented boarding school for
learning disabled or underachieving students.

The Orton Dyslexia Society
8600 LaSalle Road
Chester Building, Suite 382
Baltimore, MD 21286
410-296-0232

A professional and parent membership organization offering leadership and publications in language programs, all related to dyslexia.

The New York Branch of the Orton Dyslexia Society
71 West 23rd Street
New York, NY 10010
212-691-1930

The Parent Exchange
P.O. Box 1664
Hattiesburg, MS 39403
Carol Morrow, Editor

A newsletter aimed especially at parents.

TASK
100 West Cerritos Avenue
Anaheim, CA 92805-6546

A parent training and information organization.

Their World
The National Center for Learning Disabilities, Inc.
381 Park Avenue South
Suite 1420
New York, NY 10016
William Ellis, Executive Editor

A national not-for-profit organization committed to improving the lives of those affected with learning disabilities.

Threshold Program
Lesley College
29 Everett Street
Cambridge, MA 02138-2790
Dr. Arlyn Roffman, Director
    A program for young adults with learning disabilities at Lesley College with a curriculum designed for students who are motivated to continue their education after high school but who would have difficulty succeeding in a traditional college program.

Webb International Center for Dyslexia, Inc.
22 South Street
Waltham, MA 02154
Dr. Gertrude Webb, Director

The Whiteoak School
1 Coronado Drive
Springfield, MA 01104
413-747-5153
David Drake, Headmaster

Recommended Reading

The following are suggested reading materials on learning disabilities and attention deficit disorder for children, parents, and teachers. The books listed have been recommended by both parents and professionals.

Bloom, Jill, *Help Me to Help My Child*, Little, Brown, 1990.

Brown, Dale, *I Know I Can Climb the Mountain*, Mountain Books, 1994.

Fisher, Gary, and Cummings, Rhoda, *The Survival Guide for Kids with LD*, Free Spirit Publishing, 1990.

Galvin, Matthew, M.D., *Otto Learns About His Medication*, Magination Press, 1988.

Gehret, Jeanne, *I'm Somebody Too*, Verbal Images Press, 1992. (for sisters and brothers)

Gehret, Jeanne, *The Don't Give Up Kid and Learning Differences*, Verbal Images Press, 1990. (grades 1–3)

Hallowell, Edward, and Ratey, John, *Driven to Distraction*, Pantheon, 1994.

Herzog, Joyce, *Learning in Spite of Labels*, Greenleaf Press, 1994.

Kelly, Kate, and Ramundo, Peggy, *You Mean I'm Not Lazy, Stupid or Crazy?!—A Self-Help Book for Adults with Attention Deficit Disorders*, Tyrell & Jerem Press, 1993.

Kingsley, Jason, and Levitz, Mitchell, *Count Us In: Growing Up with Down Syndrome*, Harcourt Brace, 1994.

Learning Disabilities Council, *Understanding Learning Disabilities: A Parent Guide and Workbook*, 1991. Contact: Learning Disabilities Council at P.O. Box 8451, Richmond, VA 23226.

Levine, Mel, *Keeping a Head in School: A Student's Book about Learning Abilities and Learning Disorders*, Educators Publishing Services, 1990.

Miller, Nancy, *Nobody's Perfect: Living and Growing with Children Who Have Special Needs*, Paul H. Brookes, 1994.

Moss, Deborah M., *Shelly the Hyperactive Turtle*, Woodbine House, 1989. (grades 2–5)

Nadeau, Kathleen G., and Dixon, Ellen B., *Learning to Slow Down and Pay Attention*, Chesapeake Psychological Service, 1991. (grades 2–6)

Osman, Betty, *No One to Play with: The Social Side of Learning Disabilities*, Random House, 1989.

Schwarz, Judy, *Another Door to Learning*, Crossroad, 1992.

Setley, Susan, *Taming the Dragon: Real Help for Real School Problems*, Starfish Publishing, 1994.

Silver, Larry, M.D., *The Misunderstood Child*, TAB Books, 1991.

Smith, Romayne, ed., *Children with Mental Retardation: A Parent's Guide*, Woodbine House, 1993.

Smith, Sally L., *Succeeding Against the Odds*, Jeremy Tarcher, 1991.

Tuttle, Cheryl Gerson, and Paquette, Penny, *Parenting a Child with a Learning Disability*, Lowell House, 1993.

Vail, Priscilla, *Smart Kids with School Problems*, E.P. Dutton, 1987.

Weiss, Elizabeth, *Mothers Talk About Learning Disabilities: Personal Feelings, Practical Advice*, Prentice Hall, 1989.

West, Thomas, *In the Mind's Eye*, Prometheus Books, 1991.

APPENDIX D

PARENT-TO-PARENT PROGRAMS

The programs listed below in each state match "veteran" parents (those who have experience in meeting the challenges of children with special needs) with "new" parents (those just beginning the challenge or needing help with their children). Such groups provide emotional support, information about disabilities, and resources, referrals, advocacy training, and activities for other family members. There are many programs in each state, but due to space limitations we can list only one per state. Indeed, there are more than 500 parent-to-parent groups nationwide. Some groups focus on a single disability or a group of related disabilities whereas others are broader in focus. We thank the Beach Center at the University of Kansas for providing the following information. Contact them at 1-800-854-4938 for information on other groups.

ALABAMA
Parent-to-Parent
P.O. Box 1228
Auburn, AL 36831-1228
205-749-6784

ARIZONA
Pilot Parent Partnerships
2150 E. Highland
Suite 105
Phoenix, AZ 85016
602-468-3001

ARKANSAS
Parent-to-Parent
Union Station Square
Suite 412
Little Rock, AR 72201
501-375-4464

CALIFORNIA
Parent-to-Parent
N. Los Angeles Co. Regional
Center
8353 Sepulveda Blvd.
Sepulveda, CA 91343
818-891-0920

COLORADO
PEAK Integration Project
6055 Lehman Drive, #101
Colorado Springs, CO 80918
719-531-9400

CONNECTICUT
Lower Fairfield Co. Parent-to-
Parent Network
17 Lantern Circle
Stamford, CT 06905
203-329-1721

DELAWARE
Parent Information Center of
Delaware, Inc.
700 Barksdale Road
Suite 6
Newark, DE 19711
302-366-0152

DISTRICT OF COLUMBIA
Easter Seal Society
2800 13th Street, NW
Washington, DC 20009
202-232-2342

FLORIDA
Big Bend Parent-to-Parent
1940 N. Monroe Street
Tallahassee, FL 32303
904-488-7007

GEORGIA
Parent-to-Parent of Georgia,
Inc.
2939 Flowers Road South
Suite 131
Atlanta, GA 30341
1-800-229-2038
404-451-5484

HAWAII
Family Support Services
1319 Punahou Street
Bingham 211
Honolulu, HI 96826
808-973-8511

IDAHO
Parent-to-Parent
Route 3
Box 6554
Twin Falls, ID 83301
208-733-3191

ILLINOIS
Chicago Family Support Pilot
Project
20 E. Jackson Blvd.
Room 900
Chicago, IL 60604
312-939-3513

INDIANA
Parent Care
40 N. Ridgeview Drive
Indianapolis, IN 46219
317-353-0316

IOWA
Parent-to-Parent
133 Lillian
West Des Moines, IA 52501
515-682-6467

KANSAS
Families Together
P.O. Box 86153
Topeka, KS 66686
913-273-6343

KENTUCKY
Kentucky Special Parent
Involvement Network
318 Kentucky Street
Louisville, KY 40202
502-587-6935

LOUISIANA
Parent-to-Parent of Louisiana
Education and Support
Program
200 Henry Clay Avenue
New Orleans, LA 70118
504-896-9274

MAINE
Parents Helping Parents
5 Paul Street
Brunswick, ME 04011
207-725-6365

MARYLAND
Parent-to-Parent Network
160 Funke Road
Glen Burnie, MD 21146
301-222-7187

MASSACHUSETTS
Greater Boston Parent-to-
Parent
1249 Boylston Street
Boston, MA 02215
617-266-4520

MICHIGAN
Peer Support Project
1819 S. Wagner Road
P.O. Box 1406
Ann Arbor, MI 48106-1406
313-994-8168

MINNESOTA
Parents for Parents
Doctor's Professional Building
280 N. Smith Avenue
St. Paul, MN 55102
612-220-6731

MISSISSIPPI
Parents of Disabled Children
6742 Anna Avenue
Moss Point, MS 39563
601-475-6407

MISSOURI
Pilot Parents Program
P.O. Box 10984
Springfield, MO 65808
417-883-2593

MONTANA
Parents of Children with Special
Needs
School of Education
University of Montana
Missoula, MT 59812
406-542-1330

NEBRASKA
Parents Encouraging Parents
Nebraska Department of
Education
301 Centennial Mall South
Lincoln, NE 68509
402-471-2471

NEVADA
N-STEP, Nevada Specially
Trained Effective Parents
6200 W. Oakey
Las Vegas, NV 89102
702-870-7050

NEW HAMPSHIRE
New Hampshire Division of
Mental Health and
Development Services
Family Support Unit
105 Pleasant Street
Concord, NH 03301
603-271-5057

NEW JERSEY
Parents Encouraging Parents
(PEP)
ARC—Morris Chapter
P.O. Box 123
Morris Plains, NJ 07950
201-328-9750

NEW MEXICO
PRO Parent-to-Parent Network
1127 University, NE
Albuquerque, NM 87102
505-842-9045

NEW YORK
Parent-Friend: One to One
845 Central Avenue
Albany, NY 12206
518-438-8785

NORTH CAROLINA
Parents & Professionals
Together
Duke University Medical Center
Department of Pediatrics
P.O. Box 2916
Durham, NC 27710
919-684-3401

NORTH DAKOTA
Family First: Education for
Empowerment
P.O. Box 1883
Jamestown, ND 58402
701-252-2847

OHIO
Family First
360 S. 3rd Street
Suite 101
Columbus, OH 43215
614-228-4333

OKLAHOMA
Family Support Project
7427 E. 67th Place
Tulsa, OK 74133
918-744-1000

OREGON
Parent-to-Parent Project
Child Service Center
Portland Public Schools
531 SE 14th
Portland, OR 97212
503-280-6377

PENNSYLVANIA
Parent-to-Parent
1001 Brighton Road
Pittsburgh, PA 15233
412-322-6008

RHODE ISLAND
PRO—Parents Reaching Out
Division of Family Health
Department of Health
75 Davis Street
Providence, RI 02863
401-277-2312

SOUTH CAROLINA
National Information
Clearinghouse for Infants with
Disabilities
CDD, Benson Building, 1st
Floor
Columbia, SC 29208
1-800-922-9234

SOUTH DAKOTA
Parent-to-Parent, Inc.
3936 S. Western Avenue
Sioux Falls, SD 57105
605-334-3119

TENNESSEE
Parents Reaching Out
203 Burlington
Nashville, TN 37215
615-297-8129

TEXAS
Project KIDS
Dallas Independent School
District
12532 Nuestra
Dallas, TX 75130
214-490-8701

UTAH
Parent-to-Parent
University of Utah Hospital
50 N. Medical Drive, Room
2368
Salt Lake City, UT 84132
801-581-2098

VERMONT
Parent-to-Parent of Vermont
1 Main Street
69 Champlain Mill
Winooski, VT 05404

VIRGINIA
Parent-to-Parent—Virginia
301 W. Franklin Street
P.O. Box 3020
Richmond, VA 23284
804-225-3876

WASHINGTON
Parent-to-Parent Support
Program
2230 8th Avenue
Seattle, WA 98121
206-461-7834

WEST VIRGINIA
West Virginia PTI
Schroath Professional Building
2nd Floor, Suite 2-1
229 Washington Avenue
Clarksburg, WV 26301
304-624-1436
(There was no listing for a
Parent-to-Parent group in West
Virginia. Call the Parent
Training and Information
Program at the number above
for referral information.)

WISCONSIN
Parent-to-Parent Committee—
ARC
611 E. Wells
Milwaukee, WI 53202
414-272-2412

WYOMING
Wyoming PIC
5 N. Lobban
Buffalo, WY 82834
307-684-2277
(There was no listing for a
Parent-to-Parent group in
Wyoming. Call the number
above for referral information.)